...ng with travellers a wealth of experience and a passion for travel.

Rely on Thomas Cook as your travelling companion on your next trip and benefit from our unique heritage.

Thomas Cook **pocket** guides

TIRANA

Thomas Cook

Your travelling companion since 1873

Written by Tim Clancy & Jeroen van Marle, updated by Jeroen van Marle

Published by Thomas Cook Publishing
A division of Thomas Cook Tour Operations Limited
Company registration no. 3772199 England
The Thomas Cook Business Park, Unit 9, Coningsby Road,
Peterborough PE3 8SB, United Kingdom
Email: books@thomascook.com, Tel: +44 (0) 1733 416477
www.thomascookpublishing.com

Produced by Cambridge Publishing Management Limited
Burr Elm Court, Main Street, Caldecote CB23 7NU
www.cambridgepm.co.uk

ISBN: 978-1-84848-442-9

© 2008 Thomas Cook Publishing
This second edition © 2011 Thomas Cook Publishing
Text © Thomas Cook Publishing
Maps © Thomas Cook Publishing/PCGraphics (UK) Limited
Transport map © Communicarta Limited

Series Editor: Karen Beaulah
Production/DTP: Steven Collins

Printed and bound in Spain by GraphyCems

Cover photography © Peter Forsberg/Alamy

All rights reserved. No part of this publication may be reproduced, stored in a retrieval system or transmitted, in any form or by any means, electronic, mechanical, recording or otherwise, in any part of the world, without prior permission of the publisher. Requests for permission should be made to the publisher at the above address.

Although every care has been taken in compiling this publication, and the contents are believed to be correct at the time of printing, Thomas Cook Tour Operations Limited cannot accept any responsibility for errors or omissions, however caused, or for changes in details given in the guidebook, or for the consequences of any reliance on the information provided. Descriptions and assessments are based on the authors' views and experiences when writing and do not necessarily represent those of Thomas Cook Tour Operations Limited.

CONTENTS

INTRODUCING TIRANA
Introduction 6
When to go 8
The Human Rights Film
  Festival 12
History 14
Lifestyle 16
Culture 18

MAKING THE MOST OF TIRANA
Shopping 22
Eating & drinking 24
Entertainment
  & nightlife 28
Sport & relaxation 32
Accommodation 34
The best of Tirana 40
Suggested itineraries ... 42
Something for nothing .. 44
When it rains 46
On arrival 48

THE CITY OF TIRANA
Northside 58
Southside 74
Green Tirana 88

OUT OF TOWN TRIPS
Kruja 102
Berat 114

PRACTICAL INFORMATION
Directory 126
Emergencies 136

INDEX 138

MAPS
Tirana 50
Northside 60
Southside 76
Green Tirana 90
Kruja & Berat 104

POCKET GUIDES

SYMBOLS KEY
The following symbols are used throughout this book:

ⓐ address ⓣ telephone ⓕ fax ⓦ website address
ⓔ email ⓞ opening times ⓘ important

The following symbols are used on the maps:
- ✈ airport
- ✚ hospital
- police station
- ▤ railway station
- ✝ cathedral
- *i* tourist information centres
- ❶ numbers denote featured cafés & restaurants
- point of interest
- O city
- o large town
- ○ small town
- = motorway
- — main road
- — minor road
- — railway

Hotels and restaurants are graded by approximate price as follows:
£ budget price **££** mid-range price **£££** expensive

Abbreviations used in addresses:
Rr.   Rruga (Street)
Blvd. Bulevardi (Boulevard)

❍ *Colourful apartments in downtown Tirana*

INTRODUCING
Tirana

INTRODUCING TIRANA

Introduction

Tirana is one of Europe's youngest capital cities. Although it was originally founded in the early 17th century during the Ottoman rule of Albania, it wasn't until the early 1920s that its modern structure began to take shape. The Italian annexation of the country in 1939 was hardly good news for Tirana's inhabitants, but it did have an upside: the architects and planners sent in by Mussolini designed the grandiose boulevards and most of what is still the administrative centre in and around the city's heart, Sheshi Skënderbeu (Skanderbeg Square).

Indeed, external influences have made a significant impact on the city's character. A history of turmoil and poverty has resulted in large emigrant-Albanian communities being founded all over Europe and North America. The experiences they fed back to their families in Albania have combined with the influences of immigrant groups to give Tirana a cosmopolitan complexion that may well surprise those who regard it as the capital of an almost pathologically insular former Communist state. Visitors will now find that countless new restaurants, cafés, clubs and shops are springing up, and that there's a young generation of Albanians ready, willing and able to speak a range of major European languages, particularly Italian, English and German.

It is undeniable, though, that Albania's legacy as one of the poorest and most isolated Communist regimes is evident in its capital's infrastructure: occasional electricity shortages, the outskirts' decaying neighbourhoods and one of Europe's least developed road systems are weighing heavily on the city's ambitions of development.

INTRODUCTION

Tirana is regarded as 'neutral territory' between the tribal divides of Albania's two main clans, the Ghegs of the north and the Tosks of the south. Whereas most Albanians tend to fall into one clan or the other, Tiranians proudly claim to be the occupants of the middle ground, and their attitude somehow cements the solidarity that is innate in their national identity. In many ways the city is blazing a trail for the new Albania. It naturally assumes the mantle of cultural, political and economic hub and, according to some estimates, over half of the country's total population has gravitated towards this sprawling centre.

Tirana is a city in a state of transformation. Long isolated from European cultural currents due to the tight rule of Communist leader Enver Hoxha, this small Adriatic capital is now experiencing change at a pace unseen since the end of World War II. The streets and buildings may still be a little gritty and dusty, but Tirana is a city on the rise.

● *Tirana is a cosmopolitan city with a vibrant café culture*

INTRODUCING TIRANA

When to go

With its natural beauty and capacity for delivering constant surprises, Tirana is a fantastic destination at any time of the year but especially in spring and autumn.

SEASONS & CLIMATE

Tirana's location only 30 km (19 miles) from the Adriatic Sea means that a mild Mediterranean climate dominates the city, despite the potentially cooling influences of Mount Dajti from the east. Summers are hot and humid, particularly in July and August, but the mountains often provide balm in the form of cool evenings. If you are visiting during those hot summer months, be sure to double-check that your accommodation has air-conditioning and a generator (electricity shortages are quite common).

Winter is a bit foggy (or even smoggy) at times, but is also rather mild, with temperatures rarely falling below zero. The highlands of Dajti, on the other hand, will often be covered in snow and offer ideal conditions for the donning of snow shoes. Indeed, temperatures in the city often hover in the mid-teens°C (around 60°F), especially in the early stages of the season, when most of Tirana's rainfall occurs.

Two of the most popular times to visit are spring and early autumn. The weather is warm and extremely comfortable during these seasons, and thus the outdoor café culture is in full swing, with pleasant breezes wafting in from the Adriatic. Exploring the city on foot during these times of year makes the Tirana experience a much more enjoyable one. The intense greens and blossoms of springtime definitely contribute to the lively atmosphere that

WHEN TO GO

takes hold from April to June. The cooler autumn temperatures of September and October are a welcome relief from the late summer heat and create a similar feel to that of the onset of spring.

▲ Tirana's leafy parks are pleasant on a sunny spring day

INTRODUCING TIRANA

ANNUAL EVENTS
March
Human Rights Film Festival An inspiring product of the country's nascent human rights movement (see page 12). ❶ (04) 236 5188 ⓦ www.ihrffa.net

Summer Day With roots in a pagan festival, the 14th of March is celebrated in Tirana and Elbasan as the start of the summer. People eat special *ballokume* biscuits and the streets and squares are closed off to traffic as the crowds enjoy live music and stroll up and down the main boulevards.

May & June
Tirana Jazz Festival Although not quite on a par with many of the region's jazzborees, Tirana's jazz festival is slowly making a name for itself. ⓐ Blvd. Dëshmorët e Kombit ❶ (04) 222 8528 ⓦ www.movingculture.org

September
Tirana Biennale This contemporary art festival is held every two years (next in 2011 and 2013) and aims to promote both Albanian and foreign contemporary visual art. ⓦ www.tica-albania.org ⓔ contact.ticab@gmail.com

October
Tirana Autumn Staged at one of the most agreeable times of the year and held in venues across the city, this contemporary classical music gathering attracts some of this part of the world's finest performers. For further information, contact the ISCM ❶ (3120) 344 6060 ⓦ www.iscm.org ⓔ info@iscm.org

WHEN TO GO

November
White Night The *Nata e Bardhë* or White Night festival (on the 29th of September each year) is an all-night party featuring all of the cultural institutions. Bars and clubs host parties that last until dawn, and the streets are thronged with people soaking up the atmosphere.

November & December
Tirana International Film Festival (TIFF) Albania's largest and most successful festival celebrates the genre of the short film with dozens of internationally renowned examples, as well as offerings from students and up-and-coming artists.
ⓦ www.tiranafilmfest.com

PUBLIC HOLIDAYS
New Year 1 & 2 Jan
Summer Day 14 Mar
Day of Sultan Nevruz 22 Mar
Catholic Easter Sunday 8 Apr 2012; 31 Mar 2013
Orthodox Easter 15 Apr 2012; 5 May 2013
Fitër Bajrami (Ramadan) commences 20 July 2012; 9 July 2013
Labour Day 1 May
Day of Beatification of Mother Teresa 19 Oct
Kurban Bajram (Eid-al-Adha) 26 Oct 2012; 15 Oct 2013
Independence Day 28 Nov
Liberation Day 29 Nov
Christmas Day 25 Dec

INTRODUCING TIRANA

The Human Rights Film Festival

Albania has long struggled to break the societal restraints imposed by both Hoxha's tight Communist regime (see page 14) and by ancient tribal laws. In the early 1990s, just after the fall of the Berlin Wall, a group of intellectuals and academics formed the country's first human rights group. In 2006, after the long and tumultuous transition to democracy, the **Marubi Film & Multimedia School** (MFMS, see page 30) director, Professor Kujtim Çashku, decided, with the help of friends and colleagues throughout the West, to take the whole issue of human rights in Albania to the next level.

To achieve this, Çashku intentionally targeted his university students, believing that it would be through them that the global principles of human rights would take root in a society still struggling to embrace truly democratic philosophies. The professor calculated that an academic institution was the right kind of breeding ground for the individualism, creativity and, above all, bravery that would be needed to express artistically the grave violations taking place domestically and worldwide. His judgement was sound and his ideas inspired in his students a desire to learn from the broad landscape of human experience. Çashku's idealistic model, the Universal Declaration of Human Rights, has been a vital tool not only in educating Albania's young artists but in inspiring and motivating students to reach out and learn from the suffering of others.

Now the Marubi Film & Multimedia School is among Albania's most modern and progressive arts academies, and its goals and objectives are mirrored in the repertoire of the film

THE HUMAN RIGHTS FILM FESTIVAL

festival to which it plays host every March. The Human Rights Film Festival of Tirana is now a fascinating and moving celebration of films that strive to bring to light the issues of human trafficking, war, women's and children's rights and cultural diversity. It is a great grass-roots manifestation of a desire for social justice that will certainly provide food for thought during your travels.

○ *Many of Albania's films are shot in Tirana's old film school*

INTRODUCING TIRANA

History

There are many theories concerning the derivation of the name Tirana. The most commonly held explanation is that the Ottoman feudal lord Sulejman Pasha named the city in honour of his army's conquest of the Persian capital Tehran. This view is dispelled by the evidence of the Byzantine historian Prokop, who mentions a fortification on Mount Dajti called 'Tirkan' as early as the 6th century. Another argument claims that the name came from the Greek word *tyros*, meaning dairy, and speculates that semi-nomadic mountain shepherds would gather in the valley of present-day Tirana to trade dairy products.

What is certain is that Sulejman Pasha, like many 17th-century Ottoman leaders in the Balkans, was intent on creating himself a city. He first constructed a mosque, a *hammam* (Turkish bath) and a bakery in 1614. From that modest beginning, over the next two centuries the settlement slowly expanded as a trading and agricultural centre. The fertile lands of the vast Tirana valley were used for olive groves and fed a burgeoning trade that generated significant amounts of money. However, by the turn of the 20th century, Tirana's population still only numbered 15,000, and it was the nearby conurbation of Kruja that, as Albania's traditional capital, wielded most of the political and cultural clout. That was about to change.

In 1925 Tirana became the permanent capital. During World War II, despite fierce Partisan resistance, the city was occupied first by the Italians and later by Nazi Germany. It was liberated in 1944 when the strict regime of Enver Hoxha tightened its grip on all of Albania. Post-World War II growth was clearly marked by Soviet architectural design until, after a tiff with the Soviets, many of Tirana's grandiose museums and palaces were completed with Chinese assistance. Hoxha kept Albania under lock and key until his death in 1985. It wasn't until the collapse of the Berlin Wall that the country began to open its doors, and in 1991 student demonstrators tore down a 10-m (33-ft)-high statue of the old dictator in Skanderbeg Square. The rest of the 1990s was marked by a sketchy period of 'democratisation' and the rise and fall of corrupt governments from both the left and right. It wasn't until after the Kosovo crisis of 1999 that Tirana and Albania began to settle down and experience steady growth and rule of law. Over the past ten years stability, constantly high economic growth figures and visa liberalisation have moved Albania ever closer to its goal of European Union membership. However, the whiff of corruption permeating all political parties and the gridlock that has crippled parliament since a disputed election in 2009 are proving a serious hinderance to the country's progress.

Unknown Partisan Monument

INTRODUCING TIRANA

Lifestyle

Albanians are early risers, and the city teems with people on their way to work as early as 06.30 in the morning. But the general rule here is: take it easy. The Albanians enjoy chilling out while sipping coffee and chatting. Evening walks are also a popular pastime, particularly in the quieter neighbourhoods around **Blloku** (the Block, see page 74) and both **Parku I Madh** (Grand Park, see page 93) and **Parku Rinia** (Youth Park, see page 63).

One peculiarity that may strike the visitor is the electricity supply, which can be unreliable, especially in summer. In recent years the situation has improved, but one long, dry spell can affect the level of the lakes feeding the country's hydropower plants, leading to shortages – especially when everyone turns their new air-conditioning units on at the same time. Most hotels, restaurants and offices do have generators, but many people have become used to the lack of electricity – which sometimes also

● *Old and young on the streets of Tirana*

LIFESTYLE

⬤ *There are plenty of cafés in which to relax and soak up the atmosphere*

affects the domestic water supply – creating difficult and annoying conditions for Tirana's residents.

Although Albanians are very social and enjoy spending time with friends and family in cafés, bars and restaurants, they tend not to be extravagant in their way of life. With most growing up in relative poverty (or at least feeling the fiscal restraints of Hoxha's regime), the people of Tirana lead modest lives. On the other hand, Albanians will be extremely generous and hospitable towards visitors and foreigners, often insisting on treating their guests as honoured ones.

There is also a sharp contrast between the natives and the massive influx of migrants from the rural areas of Albania. Despite a strong sense of national identity, Tirana folk tend to be a tad sensitive towards what they call the 'rural invasion' of their city. However, the younger generations are quickly dispelling that tendency towards insularity and openly embracing the Western-oriented attitudes that have gained currency since the turn of the millennium.

INTRODUCING TIRANA

Culture

Although Tirana is relatively young in comparison with some of the country's ancient settlements, the core of the cultural scene gravitates around the capital, which contains a large number of museums and influential establishments. Much of Tirana's architecture is from the Hoxha era, and many of the beautiful buildings from Tirana's earliest days have received much-needed facelifts. The Italian-designed administrative centre and some of the Ottoman-era buildings have also been restored. For example, the **Sali Shijaku Ethnological Museum** and art gallery (see page 68) is housed in one of the city's best-preserved Ottoman homes.

A small but thriving music scene offers a wide range of genres in clubs, restaurants and official venues, though its development is slightly difficult to follow due to the severe lack of live-appearance information. The **Tirana Café Trio** band is perhaps the most famous Albanian family group, playing a dazzling array of classical, jazz, blues and new age ditties. They may be challenging to track down, but they're well worth the effort.

Pallati i Kulturës (Palace of Culture, see page 67) in Skanderbeg Square is home to the opera and ballet houses, which frequently stage performances. Culture buffs should note, though, that it's rare for shows to be presented in English. The **Galeria Kombëtare e Arteve** (National Gallery of Arts, see page 66) is Albania's most impressive arts gallery, with its rich selection of traditional and contemporary exhibitions. The Film Academy is host to southeast Europe's only **Human Rights Film Festival** (see page 12), while the **Muzeu Historik Kombëtar** (National Museum of History,

One of the famous frescoes in the Onufri National Museum (see page 120)

INTRODUCING TIRANA

● *The mosaic façade of the National Museum of History*

see page 67) is the largest cultural venue in Albania, with a large collection of historical and ethnological displays.

A common theme found throughout Albanian cultural heritage derives from a long history of resistance, and visitors may well notice a sometimes dramatic national pride among its people. This is expressed in almost every art form and is epitomised by Albania's national hero, Gjergj Kastrioti Skënderbeu, aka Skanderbeg (1404–68). Many of the bulky statues that are dotted around the place are dedicated to this icon of freedom, who fended off the invading and far superior Ottoman armies an amazing 24 times. It wasn't until Skanderbeg's death that the Ottomans were able to capture the citadel at **Kruja** just outside Tirana (see page 106). It is this spirit of self-determination and rule that defines Albania and its people and infuses its culture.

◗ *Skanderbeg Square, the heart of the city*

MAKING THE MOST OF
Tirana

MAKING THE MOST OF TIRANA

Shopping

Tirana still has a way to go in terms of creating attractive shopping venues. There is no lack of Western-name boutiques and shops – but their prices are generally no cheaper than in Western Europe. **Blloku** (see page 74), the former residential area of Hoxha and his lackeys, has a plethora of nice shops. Jewellers here tend to sell top-quality gold and silver at very reasonable prices, so you might consider splashing out on some bling from the group of establishments on Bulevardi Gjergj Fishta. Just outside the **National Museum of History** (see page 67) is a handful of souvenir shops – although many of the items on offer are mass produced and frankly uninspiring, there are a few nice and practical gifts to be found.

Albania's manufacturing industry came to a grinding halt in the late 1990s and has been slow to recover, leaving few locally produced goods worth buying. There are, however, fabulous second-hand markets scattered throughout the city, with impressive antiques and relics from the early 20th century. They may be difficult to find but the

● *Handmade carpets are a tradition dating back to Ottoman times*

SHOPPING

Tirana Backpacker Hostel (see page 39) offers a unique tour of such potential treasure troves. Whether you're an antiques collector or just curious to check out some of the great bargains, this is definitely one of Tirana's most creative and educational tours. Ask the guide to help you bargain with the vendors.

Handicrafts in Tirana are a little hard to come by, but can be found at some local markets or at a handful of artisan shops in town. A **coppersmiths shop** run by the Berhami family (❸ Rr. Hoxha Tahsim) sells well-made, authentic goods. The **bazaar** in Kruja, Albania's most famous (see page 107), is just an hour from Tirana, and has a great selection of handmade goods, ranging from carpets, handbags and wooden boxes to Albania's famous plum brandy and statues of Skanderbeg.

USEFUL SHOPPING PHRASES

How much is this?
Sa kushton?
Sah koosh-ton?

Do you have anything cheaper?
A keni ndonjë më të lirë?
A kayni nn-donya meh teh lireh?

Can I pay with a credit card?
A pranoni karta krediti?
A prah-noni karta kray-diti?

MAKING THE MOST OF TIRANA

Eating & drinking

A consequence of Albania's long history of poverty is that its cuisine tends to be quite simple. Simple is of course not a disparaging term: Albanian meat specialities are delicious, and the locals are understandably fond of their lamb dishes in particular. *Tavë kosi* is an especially tasty meal of baked lamb covered in an egg-and-yoghurt sauce. *Shishqebab* (cubes of meat – usually lamb or veal – grilled on a skewer) is a ubiquitous favourite, too. Don't be shy when it comes to inquiring about local specialities as many restaurant owners are from different parts of the country and offer interesting variations on local dishes.

The wider geographical region has also asserted its influence on Tirana. Italian food – proper Italian food – can be found in many places throughout the city. Some places even boast that Albanian mozzarella cheese is superior to the *mozzarella di bufala* from the Naples area. The Turkish-style *byrek* (a sort of pie with cheese, or sometimes spinach or potato) is a tasty and inexpensive lunch and is often accompanied by a yoghurt drink. There are also a handful of Turkish restaurants serving exquisite meals from all areas of the old empire.

> **PRICE CATEGORIES**
> The following categorisation is based on the average price per head for a two-course dinner, excluding drinks.
> £ less than 700 lek   ££ 700–1,500 lek   £££ more than 1,500 lek

EATING & DRINKING

Fresh grilled meat is a local favourite

MAKING THE MOST OF TIRANA

Tirana's centre has also seen an improvement in its 'exotic' restaurants. There's a healthy choice of Greek eateries and the city is like any other European capital in that it has several Chinese options.

Desserts in Albania stem from two sources: the Turkish/Greek influence and the Italian. The more traditional puddings like *bakllava*, *kadaif* and *hallva* were introduced during Ottoman times. It should be noted that Albanians aren't big dessert eaters, though that should by no means prevent you from indulging!

While there is certainly no shortage of Italian wines to sample here, Albania has a great selection of good-quality domestic labels. The **Çobo Winery** (see page 117) from **Berat** in the south (see pages 114–24) makes a fabulous, award-winning red from the Kashmer Albanian grape and a white Mesi i Urave. The Korça wines of Merlot and Tokay are also more than worth a sip.

Aside from the growing wine selection, the alcohol of choice for most Albanians is *raki* – an equivalent to grappa, schnapps or *shlivovitz*. Albanian *raki* is mainly produced from grapes and plums, but can also be distilled from pears, apples and mulberries in the rural areas. Albanian brandy, called *konjak*, is sold in many souvenir shops under the Skënderbeu label. Ask the vendor for the better quality variety – the larger bottles tend to be the cheap stuff while the smaller bottles, costing a bit more, contain a far classier brandy.

EATING & DRINKING

USEFUL DINING PHRASES

Please
Ju lutem
You loo-tem

Thank you
Faleminderit
Fa-lem-en-derit

The menu please!
Menynë ju lutem!
May-newe you loo-tem!

I don't eat meat/fish/dairy
Nuk ha mish/peshk/bulmet
Nook ha meesh/peshk/bool-met

Could I have the bill please?
Me bëni llogarinë ju lutem?
Meh beh-ni lo-ga-rineh you loo-tem?

Breakfast
Mëngjesi
Men-jess-ee

Lunch
Dreka
Dray-kah

Dinner
Darka
Dark-ah

Water
Ujë
Ooh-yeh

Sparkling water
Ujë me gaz
Ooh-yeh may gaaz

Still mineral water
Ujë mineral pa gaz
Ooh-yeh mean-er-al pah gaaz

Beer
Birrë
Beer-re

Wine
Verë
Vair-reh

Coffee
Kafe
Kah-fay

Tea
Çaj
Chai

Bread
Bukë
Boo-keh

Salt
Kripë
Cree-peh

Sugar
Sheqer
She-sher

MAKING THE MOST OF TIRANA

Entertainment & nightlife

If it's nocturnal entertainment you're after, look no further than **Blloku** (aka 'Bllok' or 'Block' see page 74). Hoxha's former private playground is now open to all, and you certainly don't need to fight for your right to party here. The entire neighbourhood is lined with cafés, clubs, bars and restaurants. Many of Tirana's live-music venues are here as well, with local bands playing throughout the week. Soft jazz and rock are the most common live music found, with **Charl's Bistro**

ENTERTAINMENT & NIGHTLIFE

(see page 86) and **Lollipop** (see page 87) in Blloku and **Tirana Rock** (see page 87) on Rr. Elbasanit leading the way.

The city centre also has a healthy selection of jumping bars and laid-back lounges, such as **Imagine** (see page 73) and the **Living Room** (see page 73). In summertime the relative smokiness of the venues isn't so much of a problem as you can easily get into the open air. Late at night, however, cafés and bars do tend to get rather smoggy, despite a law introduced in 2007 banning smoking in public places.

◯ *Visit the Palace of Culture for opera, ballet and the National Theatre*

MAKING THE MOST OF TIRANA

There are two cinemas that play (though not exclusively) English-language films with Albanian subtitles. **The Millennium 2** (@ Rr. Murat Toptani ☎ (04) 225 3654) is the city's main venue for local films, while the **Imperial Cinemas** chain (☎ (04) 80 45 95) has outlets in the **Sheraton Mall** (@ Sheshi Italia) and, further from the centre, in the **Kristal Center Mall** (@ Rr. Frang Bardhi). With tickets ranging from 200–700 lek, depending on the day and time, a trip to the movies offers good-value night-time entertainment. The **Marubi Film & Multimedia School** (@ Rr. Aleksandër Moisiu 76 ☎ (04) 236 5188 ⓦ www.afmm. edu.al), host of the Human Rights Film Festival (see page 12), has free foreign film screenings every Thursday night except in summer and will often show the classics that are these days only found on small screens at home.

There is a strong tradition of theatre and opera in Tirana. The **Teatri Kombëtar** (**National Theatre** @ Rr. Sermedin Said Toptani ☎ (04) 222 3022), built in honour of Mussolini in the early 1940s, has year-round performances of the works of classical playwrights and contemporary Albanian artists, with foreign-language performances dotted throughout the

> ### WHAT'S ON?
> Finding information about events is difficult in Tirana; ask at the Tourist Office, keep your eyes peeled for posters on the streets, pick up a copy of Tirana's English-language newspaper *The Tirana Times*, or check the Facebook pages of the main nightlife venues to discover what's on.

ENTERTAINMENT & NIGHTLIFE

year. Most of Tirana's classical music concerts are held in the **Academy of Arts** (( ) (04) 225 9667) on the south side of town in **Mother Teresa Square** (see page 78).

● *The Block district hosts Tirana's most happening live-music venues*

Sport & relaxation

SPECTATOR SPORTS
Football
For football fans, there is always **KF Tirana** (w www.kftirana.info) – 20-time Albanian champions. They play at the **Stadiumi Selman Stërmasi** (t (04) 223 3299), just west of the Blloku area. Tickets are more than affordable and the atmosphere is quite electric. Don't expect Premier League quality, but the level of football is still pretty decent.

PARTICIPATION SPORTS
Hiking, biking & walking
The artificial lake in the **Grand Park** (see page 93), located just behind the Sheraton Hotel on the south side of the main boulevard, is a favourite spot for long walks, cycling, jogging and fitness trails. It is an easy and safe place to get out in the fresh air.

But why not take advantage of some natural beauty? What better place for bracing exercise than **Mount Dajti** (see page 92)? And that's not all: in the village of **Ibë** (see page 88), a mere 20 minutes from the city centre and a shade past **Petrela Castle** (see page 95), there are walking trails to a cave along the crystal clear Ibë River.

Outdoor Albania (a Rr. Elbasanit 85 t (04) 222 7121 f (04) 222 7121 w www.outdooralbania.com) arranges daily walks and hikes in and around Tirana. This young organisation has pioneered the eco- and responsible tourism movement in Albania, and its members' knowledge of the terrain, friendly and professional customer service and inspired selection of activities make

SPORT & RELAXATION

outdoor sports a real pleasure. As there is a general lack of information or a tourist-friendly infrastructure for open-air activities here, many find it easier to make arrangements through a local tour operator.

RELAXATION
Swimming, saunas & gyms
The **Aquadrom Swimming Pool Complex** (@ Grand Park ⓣ (04) 225 6257 ⓞ May–Oct) has four large swimming pools and offers free locker and shower services. Several hotels – such as the Sheraton – have modern fitness centres that are free to guests.

● *KF Tirana fans enjoy a match*

MAKING THE MOST OF TIRANA

Accommodation

Tirana has a growing number of hotels of all ratings. Service, cleanliness and price can differ drastically, even in places with the same or similar ratings. **Albania Holidays** (e Rv. Sami Frasheri 20 t (04) 223 5688 or 223 5498 f (04) 223 5498 w www.albania-holidays.com) provides a reliable service, discounted room bookings and quick responses to inquiries or problems guests may experience. The website is excellent for recommendations and reservations. **Albania Experience** (e Sheraton Hotel, Sheshi Italia t (04) 227 20 55 w www.albania-experience.al) is a travel agency that also handles hotel reservations throughout Albania.

Even though there are a handful of quality 'Western' hotels, there is a growing number of very good, locally run accommodation possibilities. There is also a range of family-owned B&Bs that offer comfort, cleanliness and great prices. Going native in this way offers a much more authentic taste of Albanian hospitality and, of course, directly influences and stimulates the local economy.

> **PRICE CATEGORIES**
> Despite the fact that the lek is the local currency, all hotels in Tirana customarily list their prices in euros. This is, of course, done to attract custom from other parts of Europe.
> The following categorisation is based on the costs of a double room for one night:
> **£** less than €60   **££** €60–100   **£££** over €100

ACCOMMODATION

◆ *The Grand Hotel Tirana*

MAKING THE MOST OF TIRANA

A bedroom in the modern Green House hotel in Tirana's city centre

A number of hostels have opened in Tirana in recent years, of which **Freddy's** and the **Tirana Backpacker Hostel** (see page 39) are the most central.

HOTELS

Guva e Qetë £ A centrally located, pleasant hotel that is also home to one of Tirana's favourite bars and restaurants. The rooms all have air-conditioning, TV and phone (but no Internet). ⓐ Rr. Murat Toptani 25 ⓣ (04) 223 5491

Belvedere Dajti Tower ££ 1,420 metres above sea level at the top of the Mount Dajti cable car, this steel-and-glass hotel commands excellent views and is good for an escape from the city. ⓐ Mount Dajti ⓣ (067) 401 1035 ⓦ www.dajtitower.com

City ££ This small city centre hotel hidden in a courtyard just east of the Blloku is an excellent and affordable choice. The top floor rooms come with a terrace. ⓐ Rr. Ismail Qemali 8/1 ⓣ (04) 224 7799 ⓦ www.hotelcitytirana.com

Elysée ££ One of Tirana's more modern city-centre establishments. The rooms are pleasant, if a bit small. All have satellite TV and a mini-bar. ⓐ Rr. Themistokli Gërmenji 2/173 ⓣ (04) 222 2880 ⓦ www.hotelelysee-al.com

Vila Tafaj ££ A renovated Ottoman-era family house, this lovely hotel is centrally located. It offers friendly and helpful service that adds a homey feel to your stay. ⓐ Rr. Mine Peza 86 ⓣ (04) 222 7581 ⓦ www.tafaj.com

MAKING THE MOST OF TIRANA

Chateau Linza £££ A hilltop hotel that is just a touch out of the centre of town, located as it is near the Dajti Express cable car station (see page 92) that connects Tirana with the surrounding mountains. Now renovated, it is comfortable and spacious, with a very good restaurant that offers a panoramic view. ⓐ Qesarakë, Linze ⓣ (069) 203 0003 ⓦ www.chateaulinzahotel.com

Grand £££ A stay at the Grand involves quite a few little extras such as a sauna, indoor pool and a great roof-top bar and popular Italian restaurant. ⓐ Rr. Ismail Qemali 11 ⓣ (04) 225 3219 ⓕ (04) 224 7996 ⓦ www.grandhoteltirana.com

Green House £££ A modern hotel in the city centre, with contemporary and chic décor. The rooms are not only stylish but extremely comfortable. The restaurant serves an impressive selection of international and local cuisine and has a large, and rather popular, summer garden. ⓐ Rr. Jul Varibova 6 ⓣ (04) 222 2632

Mondial £££ Certainly one of Tirana's best Albanian-owned hotels. The service is top notch and there's a great bar and restaurant. The rooms are most agreeable, and all have satellite TV, air-conditioning, Internet and mini-bar. ⓐ Rr. Muhamet Gjollesha ⓣ (04) 223 2372 ⓕ (04) 223 2372 ⓦ www.hotelmondial.com.al

Rogner Europapark £££ Albania's best hotel, right on the main boulevard, has very comfortable rooms, a lovely tropical garden with a pool and sports facilities, and an excellent restaurant.

ACCOMMODATION

⊙ Blvd. Dëshmorët e Kombit ⊙ (04) 223 5035 ⊙ www.hotel-europapark.com

Xheko Imperial £££ Ideally located in the heart of Blloku, the Xheko Imperial hotel has lovely hardwood-decorated rooms that are comfortable and classy. It is close to the best of the city's nightlife, yet somehow manages to be a quiet place to stay.
⊙ Rr. Dëshmorët e 4 Shkurtit (on the west side of Mother Teresa Square, near the Academy of Arts) ⊙ (04) 225 9575 ⊙ (04) 224 6852 ⊙ www.xheko-imperial.com

B&BS
Friends £ Simple but clean rooms, and centrally located. Breakfast in the patisserie in front of the hotel is included.
⊙ Rr. Kavajës 86 ⊙ (04) 227 3669

HOSTELS
Freddy's Hostel £ A very comfortable hostel near Skanderbeg Square, with well-appointed and modern private rooms, each with private bathroom, TV and air-conditioning. ⊙ Rr. Bardhok Biba 75 ⊙ (04) 226 6077 ⊙ www.freddyshostel.com

Tirana Backpacker Hostel £ The best hostel in Albania. Good service, very clean, centrally located, friendly and affordable. It also offers tourist information (doubly handy in this city!), market tours and hikes with Outdoor Albania (see page 32).
⊙ Rr. Elbasanit 85 ⊙ (068) 216 7357 or (089) 211 9596
⊙ www.tiranahostel.com ⊙ Reception 08.00–22.00 daily

THE BEST OF TIRANA

Tirana offers experiences and sights that are simply not available anywhere else. You can expect anything here – anything, that is, except the old ennui.

TOP 10 ATTRACTIONS

- **Sheshi Skënderbeu (Skanderbeg Square)** Literally and spiritually the heart of the city. In Albania, all roads lead here (see page 64).

- **Architecture** Whatever flies your buttress: Ottoman, fascist, Communist – Tirana's got the lot (see page 18).

- **Sali Shijaku Ethnological Museum** A typical old Ottoman dwelling that's believed to date from the 15th century. What's more, it's the home of Sali Shijaku, one of Albania's most famous artists (see page 68).

- **Mali i Dajtit (Mount Dajti)** A cable-car ride leads to Tirana's largest recreation centre, with walking trails, restaurants, horseback riding and biking opportunities (see page 92).

- **Kalaja e Petrelës (Petrela Castle)** One of Albania's best-preserved fortifications perches picturesquely on a steep slope overlooking a river, on the road to Elbasan (see page 95).

- **Blloku (the Block)** Prior to the fall of Communism, this district was reserved solely for government officials. Today, it's the number-one spot for nightlife (see page 74).

- **Parku Rinia (Youth Park)** A welcome green area in the middle of the city; the contrast between the rural vendors selling sunflower seeds and the jet-setting coffee-sippers is typical Tirana (see page 63).

- **Muzeu Historik Kombëtar (National Museum of History)** The museum that best represents the cultural and natural heritage of Albania and its people (see page 67).

- **Pazari i Ri (Central Market)** Marketplaces are a window to the soul of any city, and Tirana's shows a fascinating combination of colours, aromas and sensations (see page 63).

- **Galeria Kombëtare e Arteve (National Gallery of Arts)** A treasure trove of over 4,000 works by Albanian and foreign artists, spanning seven centuries of cultural heritage (see page 66).

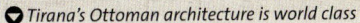
Tirana's Ottoman architecture is world class

MAKING THE MOST OF TIRANA

Suggested itineraries

HALF-DAY: TIRANA IN A HURRY
After a stroll through the impressive **Skanderbeg Square** (see page 64), head to **Blloku** (see page 74). On the way, stop at **Youth Park** (see page 63) for a coffee and snack before venturing into the once-off-limits quarters of Enver Hoxha.

1 DAY: TIME TO SEE A LITTLE MORE
Be sure to check out the **National Museum of History** in Skanderbeg Square (see page 67). The **National Gallery of Arts** (see page 66), just a few minutes' walk from the museum, hosts a fascinating collection of both antique and contemporary art. Just across the street, the **Youth Park** that was a snack-point when you only had half a day is now the perfect lunch location.

After a break, head directly across the street and give **Blloku** the time it really deserves. There are great streets to roam, shop windows to browse, pit-stop locations and linger-longer cafés. Or how about the **Sali Shijaku Ethnological Museum**, home of one of Albania's most famous artists (see page 68)? Aside from meeting the man himself and enjoying his great artwork, there's a comfortable café/restaurant in the garden of his old Ottoman home.

2–3 DAYS: TIME TO SEE MUCH MORE
After a fabulous first day following the suggestions above, use the other day(s) to explore a little outside the city centre. **Mount Dajti** (see page 92) has an excellent cable car, **Dajti Ekspres**, that takes you high above the city. When you come back to earth, the option of another 20-minute ride to **Petrela Castle** (see page 95)

SUGGESTED ITINERARIES

is a great way to end the day: cap a pleasant walk to the hilltop fortification with a drink or even a traditional meal within the stone walls. Day three unfolds just an hour from Tirana, in the historical town of **Kruja** (see pages 102–13). This is an excellent place for shopping for handicrafts in the local bazaar.

LONGER: ENJOYING TIRANA TO THE FULL

If you're fortunate enough to have time for a longer stay, be sure not to miss **Berat** (see pages 114–24), which is a two-hour drive from Tirana. You could even spend the night in this UNESCO World Heritage Site. Aside from the fascinating architecture and great views from the castle settlement above the town, there is white-water rafting available on the Osumi River in the Skrapari Canyon. This can be organised by the **Hotel Castle Park** (@ Rr. Drobonik, Berat-Përmet ❶ (032) 35 385, (067) 200 6623) or through Outdoor Albania (see page 32).

● *The ruined citadel, Berat*

MAKING THE MOST OF TIRANA

Something for nothing

Tirana is rich in opportunities to have a great time without shelling out a single, solitary lek. The **Grand Park** (see page 93) circles around a lovely artificial lake in the southern end of the city's main strip. This is an ideal place for a relaxing walk, some people-watching or just sitting on a park bench and reading a book. The locals flock there in large numbers to relax and exercise. You can, too – for free.

Markets are, thanks to their ability to produce moments of pure street theatre, highly entertaining places. The smells, colours and sounds of the **Pazari i Ri** (Central Market, see page 63) are all there for the savouring, though the tastes will probably cost you a bit. Be sure to explore thoroughly, as there are sections of the market hidden away around corners. Vendors will always allow you to try the olives, honey, fresh cheese and home-dried meats, and the *raki* stall owners will gladly let you sample the home-made brandies. Injudicious sampling could result in a free hangover.

Many people enjoy long walks through side streets and residential areas as a way of gaining deeper insight into a new city. Aside from **Skanderbeg Square**, the heart of Tirana is divided into four main neighbourhoods. Its oldest areas, **Mujos** and **Pazari**, are both on the east side of the main boulevard and divided by the **Lana River**. Many historical buildings, quaint neighbourhoods and small marketplaces off the beaten track can be discovered here. On the west side of the Dëshmorët e Kombit are two of Tirana's nicest quarters: the **Shukurit** neighbourhood on the north side of the Lana River and the tree-lined boulevards of **Blloku** just southwest of **Youth Park** (see page 63) make for some great walks.

SOMETHING FOR NOTHING

◓ *Enjoy the colours, sounds and smells at Tirana's Central Market*

Unlike the Dëshmorët e Kombit and Blloku (aka 'the Block'), where many of the chic cafés and tourist attractions are located, Shukurit gives a free taste of authentic Tirana. And even if you do decide to put your hand in your pocket, prices here will be slightly lower than in other parts of the city.

MAKING THE MOST OF TIRANA

When it rains

There are not that many large indoor venues in Tirana to cater for moist moments. But don't let that worry you: cafés are a dime a dozen and a leisurely cuppa in one of them is always a good way to pass the time. The **Blloku** neighbourhood (see page 74) is home to the cream of the city's cafés, bars and restaurants, and you'll have no trouble picking one in which to shelter.

But if significant precipitation automatically makes you yearn for a cultural refuge in which to forget about the weather, the **National Museum of History** (see page 67) is perhaps the best option. There are enough exhibitions to keep you interested for several hours, especially if you manage to hook up with an engaging guide (of which there is no shortage).

The **National Gallery of Arts** (see page 66) is always a good choice for soaking up both traditional Albanian art and the most cutting edge of the country's contemporary artistic movements. It's a popular gathering point for young people and a really good place to meet the locals. Further down Dëshmorët e Kombit boulevard is the **Archaeological Museum** (see page 81) in Mother Teresa Square. Although its displays may seem somewhat amateur, the content of some of the exhibitions is interesting and will soon make you forget inclement weather. Finally, Tirana's new shopping centres are also good for a rainy day; try the city centre **Galeria Mall** (a Blv. Bajram Curri, behind the Pyramid), **Coin** (a Rr. Papa Gjon Pali II, ABA Tower), the **Vesa Center** (a Rr. Abdyl Frashëri 5) or the huge **Citypark Albania** mall (a 8 km (5 miles) out of town along the Durrës highway), which also offers indoor skating.

WHEN IT RAINS

○ *A Roman bust in the Archaeological Museum*

MAKING THE MOST OF TIRANA

On arrival

TIME DIFFERENCE
Albania falls under the Central European Time (CET) zone, GMT+1.

ARRIVING
By air
The **Nënë Tereza Tirana International Airport** (ⓐ Rinas ⓘ (04) 222 3938, lost & found (04) 238 1681 ⓦ www.tirana-airport.com.al), 25 km (just over 15 miles) from the city centre, is a brand new modern facility. There is an ATM within the airport, visible as soon as you clear customs, as well as an occasionally manned tourist information desk. The Rinas Express Airport Bus line runs regularly to the city centre and costs 250 lek. Taxis will usually charge €20 to convey you to any destination in the city. The drive to town should take slightly over a half an hour.

By rail
There are no international trains to Albania. The country's rail system would represent a highly challenging experience to even the most devout rail enthusiast, and buses are almost always a quicker option. Despite the impossibility of arriving in the country directly by train, there are nevertheless limited internal rail lines (see page 126) which could conceivably be useful if you're entering Albania from southern Macedonia or Montenegro.

Tirana Railway Station ⓐ Blvd. Zogu I ⓘ (04) 223 6356 or 225 1094

ON ARRIVAL

Tirana's airport is convenient and modern

MAKING THE MOST OF TIRANA

ON ARRIVAL

MAKING THE MOST OF TIRANA

○ *Tirana's local buses pick up and drop off at Skanderbeg Square*

By road

As there is no official bus station, buses coming from abroad will most likely drop their passengers off on the outlying ring road, which means taking either a local city bus or a taxi to the city centre. Adventurous types who aren't fazed by the possibility of a mystery tour will be pleasantly surprised to find that most bus fares are a mere 30 lek (paid once you're on board).

Arriving by car is certainly not for the faint of heart. If you've managed to navigate your way through Europe's worst road system and have reached Tirana, you'll soon realise that the

IF YOU GET LOST, TRY...

Do you speak English?
A flisni Anglisht?
A flees-nee Anglisht?

Where is...?
Ku është...?
Coo eshte?

Where is a telephone, please?
Ku mund të marr në telefon ju lutem?
Coo moond te mar neh tay-lay-fon you loo-tem?

Excuse me, where can I get a taxi?
Ku mund të marr një taksi?
Coo moond te mar nyeh taxi?

Right	**Left**
Djathtas	Majtas
Dyath-tas	*My-tas*
Straight ahead	**After the stop light**
Drejt	Pas semaforit
Drayt	*Pass say-ma-fo-reet*

fun has only just begun. Driving in the city can be an unsettling experience, though the locals seem to have become immune to any chaos-related stress. The most practical thing you can do is to throw most of the driving rules that you use at home right out the window. Tirana traffic is rather dense, and drivers have a distinct predilection for using the horn. Lanes are, for the most part, non-existent as drivers will push and squeeze their vehicles into any open spaces. Parking is very difficult and it may not be wise to leave your car unattended overnight in an unsupervised place.

By sea

Once you've arrived at the **Port of Durrës** (❶ (052) 220 28) by ferry, the procedures are fairly straightforward. When you exit the customs area there will be a horde of taxis and mini-buses waiting. However, taxis to Tirana from Durrës will be very expensive: it's best to find a mini-bus, ordinary bus or even grasp the nettle and travel on Albania's rail network. Trains run daily from Durrës to Tirana at 06.15, 08.45, 09.20, 13.05, 16.45 and 20.05 and cost 70 lek.

FINDING YOUR FEET

Bearing in mind that the public transport system is a little primitive, it's good news indeed that a large majority of the things to see and do in Tirana are reachable on foot. As the entire city centre is flat, there are no hills or areas that are difficult to walk through. Pedestrians do need to be careful when crossing the road: green pedestrian signals don't necessarily mean that cars will stop to let you pass. Tirana is

ON ARRIVAL

generally a safe place, though you should always be careful of pickpockets, particularly if you do venture onto crowded public transport.

ORIENTATION

The challenge of orienting yourself has an extra dimension in Tirana – many Communist-era street signs have been torn down and not (yet) replaced. Happily, the boulevards and eye-catching buildings produce many handy landmarks. The main boulevard, Dëshmorët e Kombit, divides the city east and west. The **Lana River**, just south of Skanderbeg Square, marks the north–south divide and crosses Dëshmorët e Kombit at the **Youth Park** (see page 63). At the northern end of the boulevard, **Skanderbeg Square** contains landmarks such as the **Tirana International Hotel** and the **National Museum of History** (see page 67). Just south of the Lana River is the **Pyramid** (see page 79), which is a good landmark and an easy word to communicate to locals if you're lost. (For the purpose of providing a practical partition of Tirana, the City of Tirana section of this guide divides the city into Northside and Southside.)

GETTING AROUND

The public bus system runs from 06.00 to 22.00 Monday to Saturday. Although fairly regular and used by locals, it can be a little complex to understand for first-time visitors. There is no official bus station and very few public transport maps are available.

If you don't want to get around on foot (the easiest option), taxis will be the best way to move about. Drivers charge between

MAKING THE MOST OF TIRANA

300 and 500 lek for most destinations in town. It's best to ask at your hotel if the proprietors will help you to arrange a pre-set price with a reliable firm – taxis do not have meters, so it's easy for drivers to inflate rates. The yellow taxis are the only licensed ones in Tirana and are highly recommended.

Radio Taxi (04) 224 4444, 237 7777, 225 5555, 225 1500, 225 8888 or (068) 222 5657

Car hire

If you've decided to take on the Albania driving challenge, there are several reliable car-hire agents in Tirana. Expect to pay a minimum of €45 per day (prices are charged in euros) for basic cars. In addition to the offices listed below, Avis and Hertz also have desks at the airport.

Avis ⓐ Rogner Hotel, Blvd. Dëshmorët e Kombit (04) 23 50 11 (04) 23 50 24 www.avis.al/eng 08.30–18.30 Mon–Sat, closed Sun

Budget ⓐ Rr. Elbasanit, Nd. 10, H.5 (04) 450 5555 (04) 450 5555 www.budget.com 08.00–18.00 Mon–Fri, 09.00–15.00 Sat, closed Sun

Europcar ⓐ L.61, Rr. e Durrësit (04) 222 7888, (038) 203 9708 (04) 224 6192 www.europcar.com 08.00–18.00 daily

Hertz ⓐ Tirana International Hotel, Skanderbeg Square (04) 223 5109 www.hertz.com 08.00–19.00 Mon–Fri, 08.00–16.00 Sat, closed Sun

◉ *The Lana River separates the Northside and Southside*

THE CITY OF
Tirana

THE CITY

Northside

The north side of Tirana is where most of the city's cultural institutions and main squares are. The bulk of the museums and interesting monuments will be found in the old **Pazari** neighbourhood, to the east of the main **Skanderbeg Square** (see page 64).

SIGHTS & ATTRACTIONS

Et'hem Bey Mosque

The Et'hem Bey Mosque, although not the oldest in Tirana, is one of the most important Islamic buildings in Albania and a protected national monument. Exact figures regarding Tirana's Muslim population are disputed, but many of those who are practising Muslims belong to the Bektashi order of dervishes (see page 107). Located in the heart of Skanderbeg Square, this is the only religious building in the area to have survived the Communist purge of sacral objects. Construction is believed to have lasted over a quarter of a century, having been initiated by Mula Bey in 1794. By the early 1820s, his son Selim (the great-grandson of Sulejman Pasha) had finished his father's work. The mosque was built in traditional Ottoman style, which is also found in other Balkan capitals like Skopje and Sarajevo. Several restorations have taken place over the past century but the mosque has largely maintained its original appearance.

ⓐ Skanderbeg Square ⓣ (04) 222 3701 ⓒ 08.00–22.00 daily (summer); 08.00–19.00 daily (winter) ⓘ If you arrive during one of the five daily prayer sessions, it's best to come back later

NORTHSIDE

○ *Et'hem Bey Mosque*

THE CITY

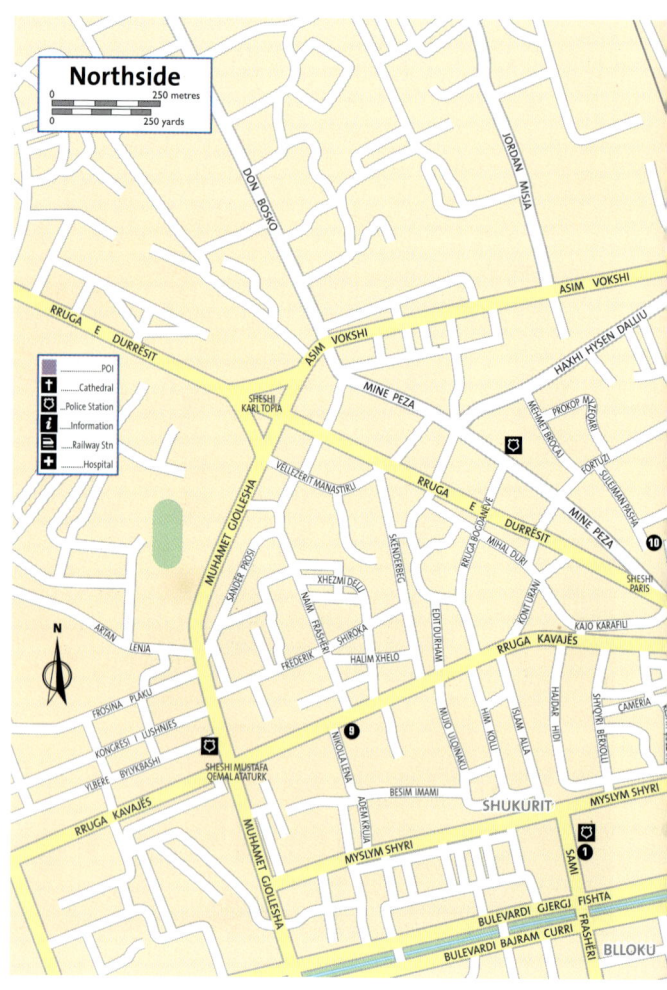

NORTHSIDE

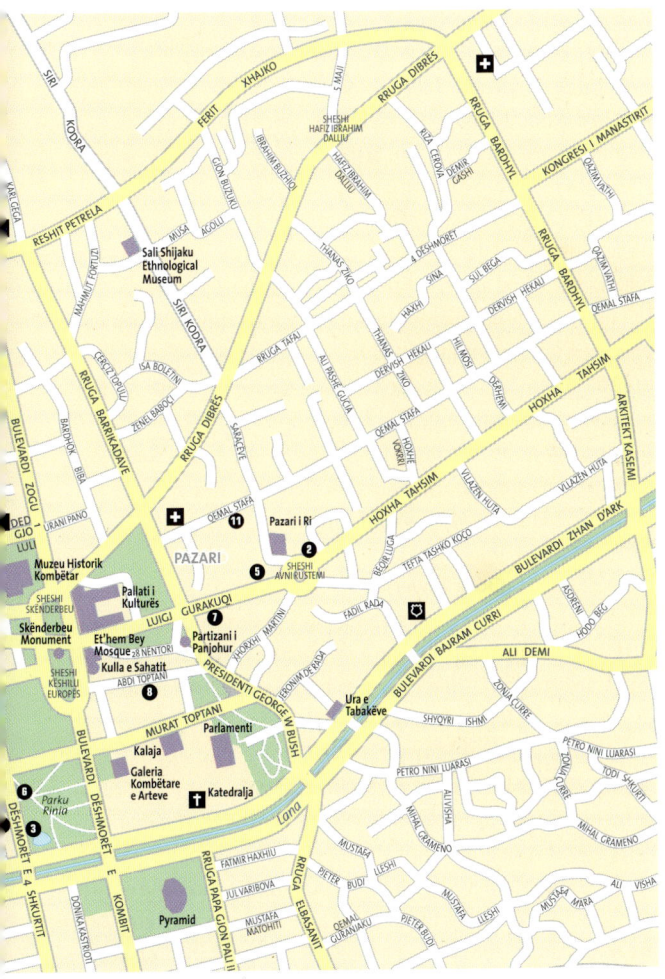

THE CITY

Kalaja (Fortress of Justinian)

Tucked behind the rows of imposing buildings that line Dëshmorët e Kombit, Kalaja is located in Tirana's oldest neighbourhood. Kalaja is believed to have been a fortified Byzantine settlement in the 6th century, built at the behest of the emperor Justinian, and clearly played a significant role in ruling the areas in and around the present-day city. The Ottomans, under Sulejman Pasha, expanded the fortress in the 17th century, adding a cultural and commercial trade centre. In the early 1800s, the powerful Toptani family from Kruja took control and Kalaja was even further enhanced with two Ottoman-style homes that are still standing. The city's civic leaders have big plans for the fortress, but, tantilisingly, it is not yet open to the public. Only the ancient walls that line Murat Toptani Street and some recently excavated foundations are viewable, and they are impressive enough. ⓐ Rr. Murat Toptani

Kulla e Sahatit (Clock Tower)

Clock towers were always significant Islamic symbols during Ottoman times, and this is no exception. It was built in the 1820s next to the Et'hem Bey Mosque by Haxhi Et'hem Bey and the well-to-do Tufina family. The original clock was replaced and its tower raised to 35 m (115 ft) in 1928. It was partially destroyed during World War II, however, and, once again, a new clock had to be fitted. Today the tower, although flanked by the many large Socialist-era buildings that pepper Skanderbeg Square, is one of the most central and recognisable objects in the entire city. Should you decide to ascend – and you should, as the views are remarkable – be prepared for a spiralling climb of 90 steps.

NORTHSIDE

 Skanderbeg Square (next to Et'hem Bey Mosque) (04) 224 3292
 09.00–13.00, 16.00–18.00 Mon, Wed & Sat, closed Tues, Thur & Fri, Sun Admission charge

Parku Rinia (Youth Park)
At the beginning of the 21st century, Parku Rinia more resembled a chaotic improvised market than the lovely and popular park it is today. Comprehensively made-over, it's become one of Tirana's most popular destinations for both locals and tourists. In pleasant weather the park positively teems with frolickers of every age and provenance. It's a great place to sit and people-watch or simply read a book. Towards the rear section of the park are a video arcade, a restaurant and a café that's situated alongside a cooling water fountain. Blvd. Dëshmorët e Kombit 24 hrs

Partizani i Panjohur (Unknown Partisan Monument)
Just past the Kaplan Pasha monument is a square, usually crowded with men sitting on its steps playing draughts. Above them is the large and triumphant tribute to unknown partisans who fell in World War II. Rr. Punëtorët e Rilindjes

Pazari i Ri (Central Market)
One way to experience the real Tirana is to invest just a few minutes wandering around the Pazari i Ri. The Central Market is a great place to meander, mingle, take photos, hunt for bargains and try some of Albania's delightful rural products. The country is famous for its olives and is, in fact, the world's largest exporter of wild sage. The traditional cheeses from countryside areas are also worth a

THE CITY

taste test. The main square contains stalls selling more souvenir-type objects, but for the really authentic food markets be sure to explore all the little side streets. ❷ Just off Sheshi Avni Rustemi ❶ (04) 222 5287 ❶ 08.00–14.00 daily

SHESHI SKËNDERBEU (SKANDERBEG SQUARE)

Named after Albania's most revered hero, Skanderbeg, all roads into and out of the city converge here. The square existed well before World War II, but it was during Hoxha's era that its vast expansion really began, and – make no mistake – this is the focal point of Tirana. Its large, wide cobblestone boulevards are lined with Albania's most significant cultural, historical, political and administrative buildings.

Beside the Ottoman-era **Et'hem Bey Mosque** (see page 58) and the early 20th-century Italian architecture of the town hall and the national bank towards the southern end of the square, most of the urban furniture is a melange of Soviet, Chinese and Albanian socialist styles; the **National Museum of History** to the northwest of the square (see page 67) is by far the most visible building here. The **Skanderbeg Monument**, erected in 1968 on the 500th anniversary of the iconic figure's death, is often surrounded by pensioners and those who are between jobs. At the time of writing, the square was mercifully closed to traffic in preparation for an ambitious renovation project that will see it become a fully pedestrianised area with trees and fountains – hopefully a vibrant, renewed heart for Tirana.

NORTHSIDE

◆ *Tirana's town hall in Skanderbeg Square*

THE CITY

Ura e Tabakëve (Tanners' Bridge)

The Ottomans left many beautiful architectural footprints throughout the Balkans, particularly thanks to their skill in bridge design. Tanner's Bridge is one such relic. This small footbridge, which originally spanned the Lana River, once connected the highlands and foothills of Mount Dajti with Tirana, and its main function was to facilitate the trading of agricultural products and livestock. In the years leading up to World War II, though, the Lana was rerouted and the bridge fell into disuse. It has now been restored and is a popular pedestrian crossing. The café next to the bridge is not only a nice place for a coffee but perhaps the best spot for a memorable photograph. ⓐ Presidenti George W Bush intersection with Blvd. Zhan D'Ark

CULTURE

Galeria Kombëtare e Arteve (National Gallery of Arts)

The National Gallery of Arts is hands-down the best-arranged publicly operated cultural institution in Tirana. The collection of works by foreign artists may only be relatively modest, but its highlights are two most impressive permanent exhibitions of treasures from the Albanian National Renaissance and Independence period (1883–1944) and paintings and sculptures from the Socialist Realism era (1944–90). Many of the contemporary displays are excellent, and don't miss the Marubi Photograph Collection when it comes to town every year. ⓐ Blvd. Dëshmorët e Kombit ⓣ (04) 222 6033 ⓛ 09.00–13.00, 16.00–19.00 Tues–Sun, closed Mon ⓘ Admission charge

NORTHSIDE

Muzeu Historik Kombëtar (National Museum of History)

Perhaps the most recognisable building in all of Tirana, the National Museum of History is a tribute to Albania's long and rich cultural and historical heritage. The façade's massive and colourful mosaic dominates Skanderbeg Square and depicts the spectrum of Albanian history, from the indigenous Illyrian tribes to the heroic partisans of World War II.

The museum, which was built in 1981, has a similarly diverse collection of exhibitions, ranging from mid-Palaeolithic to the Hoxha era (the more contemporary exhibits are far richer and better organised than the prehistoric sections). Highlights are the ethnological display of traditional Albanian attire and the chronological story of the Illyrian tribes that once inhabited most of modern-day Albania. The most common thread running throughout the museum is the Albanians' history of resisting invaders, a theme that recurs during visits to any cultural institution here. The souvenir shop has one of Tirana's best selections of gifts, and should be borne in mind when you're on the hunt for mementos. ⓐ Skanderbeg Square ⓘ (04) 222 8389 ⓛ 09.00–12.00, 17.00–19.00 Tues–Sun, closed Mon ⓘ Admission charge

Pallati i Kulturës (Palace of Culture)

This 1960s Soviet-style building was on the point of being finished when Enver Hoxha had a falling-out with Russian leader Nikita Khrushchev. This led to the Soviets quickly leaving Albania and abandoning an incomplete Palace of Culture. Happily, Chinese experts soon arrived to save the day and rapidly completed both the palace and the present-day Tirana

THE CITY

International Hotel. Today's Palace of Culture houses both the City Opera and the National Library. The **Adrion International Bookstore** (see page 70) is on the north corner of the building.
ⓐ Skanderbeg Square

Sali Shijaku Ethnological Museum

The family home of Sali Shijaku, an Albanian artist inspired by French Impressionism but also regarded as the country's best Socialist-era realist, doubles as a terrace café and an 'ethno house' modestly decorated with pieces of his own art. It was Shijaku who sculpted the massive monument of Hoxha that once stood in Skanderbeg Square (and who was present when it was torn down). The quality of the art on display, the beauty of the restored Ottoman home and the opportunity to meet Shijaku combine to make this one of Tirana's most unique and authentic attractions. Give yourself enough time to sip a coffee, absorb the art, or even stay for lunch. ⓐ Rr. V Luarasi
ⓣ (04) 223 8343 ⓒ 08.00–20.00 daily

RETAIL THERAPY

There are several shopping areas of interest on Tirana's north side, not least the **Pazari i Ri** (Central Market, see page 63), which could well be Tirana's most unique shopping experience. Behind the **Youth Park** (see page 63), between Dëshmorët e 4 Shkurtit and Myslym Shyri, you'll find a good selection of shops, and it is well worth a stroll down the tree-lined avenues for a browse. Double back on Bulevardi Gjergj Fishta and you'll see some more fascinating shops.

Sali Shijaku Ethnological Museum

THE CITY

Adrion International Bookstore Good, if pricey, selection of English-language books about Albania. ⓐ Palace of Culture, Skanderbeg Square

Citypark Albania Tirana's largest and newest mall is 8 km (5 miles) from town along the Durrës highway. It has over 180 shops, a hypermarket, the only skating rink in the country and children's entertainment. ⓐ Durrës highway
ⓦ www.cityparkalbania.com

Lleshi Typical Albanian souvenir shop with a rich selection of Albanian folk attire. A good place to find interesting knick-knacks like carpets and knitted wool clothing. ⓐ Rr. Durrësit & Rr. Asim Vokshi

◒ *The Taiwan complex in Youth Park has a plethora of eateries and cafés*

Rreli Erebara As well as traditional souvenirs they have a nice selection of silver and bronze gifts, hand-carved wooden items and pottery. ⓐ Rr. Ded Gjo Luli

TAKING A BREAK

Friends Book House £ ❶ A 24-hour bookshop and café that's a real favourite among Tirana's literary set. The selection of English-language books and newspapers is perhaps a little limited, but it's certainly enough to enjoy a coffee and (delicious) cake over. ⓐ Rr. Sami Frashëri ⓣ (04) 226 6664 ⓛ 08.00–24.00 daily

Stephen Center Café £ ❷ Very conveniently located in the neighbourhood of the central marketplace. On offer are tasty, good-value lunches and a popular Sunday brunch. ⓐ Sheshi Avni Rustemi ⓣ (04) 223 4748 ⓛ 07.00–23.00 daily

Taiwan Café £ ❸ One of the city's most popular eateries, and – good though the snacks here are – its leading selling points are the fountains and the truly excellent coffees.
ⓐ Rr. Dëshmorët e 4 Shkurtit, Parku Rinia

La Voglia £ ❹ A café that attracts a mainly young, local crowd at lunchtime; pop on down and you'll receive a hearty welcome. The pizzas and sandwiches are tasty, the staff are English-speaking and there's a terrace that's great in the summer. ⓐ Rr. Dëshmoret e 4 Shkurtit ⓣ (04) 225 8899 ⓛ 09.00–01.00 daily

THE CITY

AFTER DARK

RESTAURANTS

Oda £–££ ❺ A lovely family run traditional restaurant in an old building near the market. Let the waiter suggest a typical Albanian meal – you won't be disappointed. ⓐ Rr. Luigj Gurakuqi ⓣ (04) 224 9541 ⓗ 11.00–23.00 Mon–Sat, 13.00–23.00 Sun

Casa di Pasta ££ ❻ The food here is almost as good as the Italian blueprints that inspired it. There's a great menu at very affordable prices, and do make sure you treat yourself to a *tres leches* (that's how they spell it) dessert! Inside the Taiwan complex. ⓐ Blvd. Dëshmorët e 4 Shkurtit, Parku Rinia ⓗ 08.00–22.00 daily

Rozafa ££ ❼ Be sure not to confuse it with its sister pizzeria around the corner. Rozafa is known for its fish specialities, and these are accompanied by the contents of a good wine list. Service is excellent. ⓐ Rr. Luigj Gurakuqi 89 ⓣ (04) 222 2786 ⓦ www.rozafa.al ⓗ 12.00–24.00 daily

Sarajet ££ ❽ One of Tirana's most beautiful restaurants. Situated in an 18th-century Ottoman house, it has a fabulous ambience. The food is generally traditional and the service is very good. Try the summer garden if the weather is nice. ⓐ Rr. Abdi Toptani ⓣ (04) 242 1284 ⓗ 07.00–23.00 daily

Sofra Turke ££ ❾ Excellent Turkish grilled meat and vegetarian dishes in a cosy restaurant. Leave room for the sticky and sweet desserts. ⓐ Rr. Kavajës 170 ⓣ (04) 222 6818 ⓑ 08.00–23.00 daily

Piazza £££ ⑩ A restaurant that consistently ranks among Tirana's best. This rather upmarket establishment has superb service, delicious food and a fresh salad bar. ⓐ Rr. Ded Gjo Luli ⓣ (04) 223 0706 ⓑ 12.00–17.00, 19.00–23.00 daily

Vinum £££ ⑪ One of Tirana's best restaurants, hidden away in an alley near the market. It's not as cheap as elsewhere but the setting in an old villa, the professional service and creative cuisine make it worth a visit. ⓐ Rr. Qemal Stafa 60 ⓣ (04) 223 0822 ⓑ 07.00–23.00 daily

CLUBS & BARS

Imagine At the side of the Tirana International Hotel, Imagine is a great live music venue with lively rock and jazz concerts every weekend. ⓐ Sheshi Skënderbeu 8 ⓣ (068) 206 1088 ⓑ 19.30–03.00 Wed–Sat

Living Room A fancy bar and rooftop restaurant that packs in the punters on multi-level terraces overlooking the city. The parties here always go on until late. ⓐ Presidenti George W Bush 16 ⓣ (067) 203 3225 ⓑ 19.00–03.00 daily

Venue Dance Club A club playing house and dance music, just a short taxi ride from the centre. ⓐ Rr. Sadik Petrela 20 ⓣ (068) 601 1111 ⓦ www.venuedanceclub.com ⓑ 22.00–04.30 Fri & Sat, closed Aug

THE CITY

Southside

South of the Lana River is an area that is a bit more upmarket than its northern neighbour. There are many ministries, the residency of the president of Albania, and the former neighbourhood of the Communist elite that's now been transformed into the trendiest nightlife and dining hotspot in Tirana. Whereas in the northern half of the city you'll find museums and a considerable number of historical attractions, the south side has the largest and best selection of cafés, restaurants, bars and clubs. This is also by far the best place in town for shopping, relaxing in the countless cafés and experiencing the atmosphere of the city's live music venues.

SIGHTS & ATTRACTIONS

Blloku (the Block)

For years this once-elite area of Tirana – also known as 'Bllok' or, to English-speakers, 'the Block' – was unseen by a large majority of the people who were born and raised in the city. Enver Hoxha and his closest Communist chums used it as their own enclosed world of privilege. Now open to all, this exciting and trendy quarter of Tirana houses its finest nightlife venues.

Hoxha's residence

There is no doubt that this place should be a museum dedicated to the good, bad and ugly of Hoxha's Communist regime. Unfortunately, the wounds from his era are slow to heal and Tirana is not yet ready to establish any kind of

SOUTHSIDE

🔺 *The Twin Towers are landmark buildings in the Block district*

THE CITY

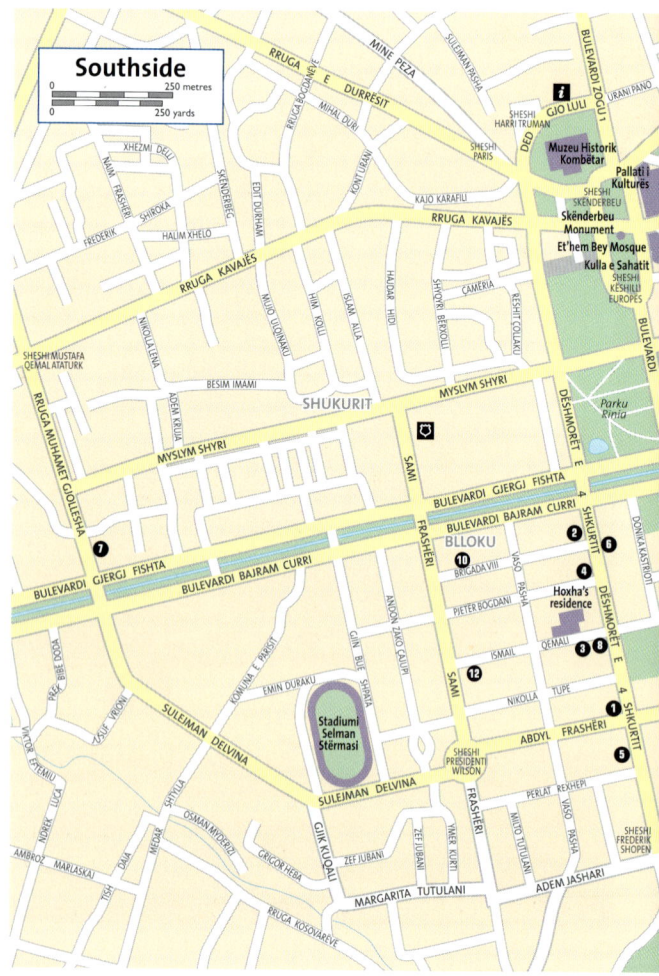

SOUTHSIDE

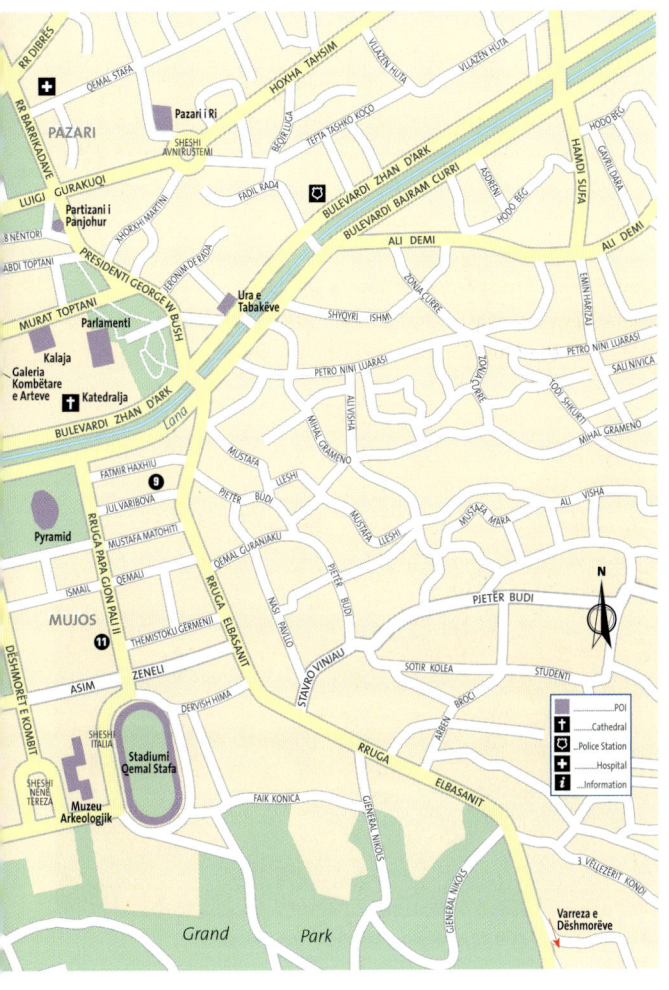

THE CITY

memorial to the man many consider to have been a brutal dictator. His residence, in the heart of Blloku, can only be viewed at a short distance from its gates. Parts of the property have been converted to cafés or offices, but the main residence still remains off-limits to visitors. Expect that to change in the future, though HoxhaLand may still be some considerable time away.
ⓐ Corner of Rr. Ismail Qemali and Rr. Vaso Pasha

Sheshi Nënë Tereza (Mother Teresa Square)

Overshadowed only by Skanderbeg, Mother Teresa is the pride and joy of the Albanian people. Although she wasn't born in

▲ *Looking north over Enver Hoxha's former house and gardens*

Albania proper, her Albanian blood is more than enough qualification to make her a revered national symbol. In contrast to the martial qualities of the warrior, the woman born Agnes Gonxhe Bojaxhiu is perceived to have embodied a spirit of compassion, peace and love. At the far southern end of Dëshmorët e Kombit is Mother Teresa Square. To some it may appear odd and over-modest: its centrepiece is a waterless fountain, though there is a statue of her in the corner beside the university building. For tourists, the square is perhaps most interesting for the **Archaeological Museum** (see page 81) and the proximity of the **Grand Park** (see page 93).

Varreza e Dëshmorëve (Martyrs' Cemetery)

Burial grounds may not be every visitor's idea of a magnetic must-see, but the Martyrs' Cemetery is most definitely worth a visit as an example of funerary architecture and design: Socialist-era cemeteries across the Balkans are impressive for their bold layout and immense size. Not only that, but it's home to one of Tirana's most impressive statues, Mother Albania, which, as its inscription proudly states, is dedicated to 'The Eternal Glory of the Martyrs of the Fatherland'. Interestingly enough, most of the Communist elite are not buried there (Enver Hoxha was dug up and transplanted to the city cemetery in 1992). Rr. Elbasanit

CULTURE

Pyramid

Formerly known as the Enver Hoxha Monument, the 'Pyramid' (as it's more popularly known) is one of Tirana's quirkiest

THE CITY

SIGNS OF THE TIMES

The uses to which the 'Pyramid' has been put in its 20-year life reflect Albania's transformation. Pranvera Hoxha designed a mausoleum fit for a pharaoh, but when Communism collapsed, her father's body was brusquely rehoused in the **Martyrs' Cemetery** (see page 79). At the moment, the building is popular as a giant slide for children.

SOUTHSIDE

landmarks. Designed by Hoxha's daughter, this expression of filial pride was the most expensive architectural venture of its time. Today, the centre stands empty, awaiting a decision on its future purpose. There are plans to demolish it, so get a snapshot while you can. ⓐ Blvd. Dëshmorët e Kombit

Muzeu Arkeologjik (Archaeological Museum)
Like many state-run museums in the Balkans, the Archaeological Museum in Tirana offers a rather fascinating collection of ancient

◯ *The Pyramid, built as Hoxha's mausoleum*

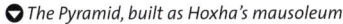

THE CITY

artefacts that are exhibited in a perhaps basic, and sometimes monotonous, way. Among the most interesting displays is the section dedicated to the Albanian national hero, Skanderbeg.
ⓐ Sheshi Nënë Tereza ⓣ (04) 224 0711 ⓛ 10.30–15.00 Mon–Fri, closed Sat & Sun

RETAIL THERAPY

Blloku is the capital's upmarket shopping zone. Many Western brand-name shops can be found here but tend to be just as, if not more, expensive than branches in the West. There are a dozen or so unique shops selling locally made jewellery, ceramics and other quality items between Vaso Pasha and Dëshmorët e 4 Shkurtit streets. There are also many shops in Tirana's new skyscrapers. It is a safe bet to try to focus any shopping frenzy on the area on the west side of Bulevardi Dëshmorët e Kombit, all the way to Rr. Sami Frashëri.

Coin A brand new shopping centre on the ground floor of the colourful ABA highrise, with Italian fashion in the OVS shop, and food available higher up in the building. ⓐ Rr. Papa Gjon Pali II, ABA Business Center Tower

Galeria A cluster of over 70 shops, located just behind the Pyramid in the European Trade Centre. ⓐ Blvd. Bajram Curri

Librari Albania Good selection of English-language books on Albania at a cheaper price than Adrion in Skanderbeg Square (see page 70). Contains most of the well-known author Ismail

Kadare's books in English translation. ⓐ Rr. Sami Frashëri
ⓦ www.albaniabook.com

Sheraton Plaza The Sheraton seems to have it all. As well as a hotel, fitness centre and cinema you'll also find a small shopping centre with a food court, cafés and nice boutiques. ⓐ Sheshi Italia

TAKING A BREAK

Juna £ ❶ Located in one of the busiest areas of Blloku near the University bookshop on the corner of Abdyl Frashëri. It's a great spot for young travellers to mix and mingle with peers. ⓐ Rr. Dëshmorët e 4 Shkurtit ⓣ (04) 225 9238 ⓛ 07.00–23.00 daily

Pasticeri Franceze £ ❷ As good as anything you'll find in Paris. The cakes and desserts are *magnifique*, as is the healthy selection of snacks and drinks. ⓐ Rr. Dëshmorët e 4 Shkurtit 1 ⓣ (04) 225 1336 ⓛ 07.00–22.00 daily

Quo Vadis £ ❸ A notably hip establishment, where the concept of the mid-afternoon coffee break has become a style statement. ⓐ Ismail Qemali 21 ⓛ 07.30–01.00 daily

Vogue Lounge £–££ ❹ This old villa in the centre of the Blloku district is now an elegant café, where the airy rooms and large terrace are perhaps the best place in town to have a coffee or cocktail and people-watch. ⓐ Rr. Dëshmorët e 4 Shkurtit ⓣ (067) 300 22 73 ⓛ 07.30–02.00 daily

THE CITY

Serendipity ££ ❺ A favourite among expats in Tirana. Just next to the Xheko Imperial Hotel, it's a good lunch place and even better for an evening out. The curries and jambalaya go down well with tourists hungry for a taste of something different. ⓐ Rr. Dëshmorët e 4 Shkurtit 26 ⓣ (04) 225 9377 ⏰ 08.00–24.00 daily

Sky Club Café ££ ❻ It's hard to find a 'bad' café in Tirana, especially in Blloku. However, few can offer what the Sky Club can. Perched on top of the 17th floor of the Sky Tower, it's a marvellous place for a light lunch or drink break and to get a bird's-eye view of the city, not to mention the rotating floor that gives you the full spectrum while sitting and sipping. This is, however, one of the pricier cafés in town. ⓐ Rr. Dëshmorët e 4 Shkurtit 5 ⓣ (04) 222 1666 ⏰ 08.00–23.00 daily

AFTER DARK

RESTAURANTS

Amor ££ ❼ With daily specials that the chef/owner decides on based on the morning's markets, you can't go wrong here. Ingredients are extremely fresh, the menu is diverse, food is excellent and the price is just right. ⓐ Rr. Muhamet Gjollesha ⓣ 069 407 8106 ⏰ 12.00–22.30, closed Sun

Carlsberg ££ ❽ Despite its name being evocative of other pleasures, this fine restaurant actually produces excellent Albanian dishes and a good range of European cuisine. The lamb dishes here are particularly scrumptious. Inside the Xheko Imperial

SOUTHSIDE

An authentic French patisserie at Pasticeri Franceze

THE CITY

Hotel. ⓐ Rr. Dëshmorët e 4 Shkurtit ⓣ (04) 224 6852
⏱ 12.00–22.30 daily

Green House ££ ❾ Here you'll find a good selection of Italian and international meals. The summer garden is an especially nice place in which to dine, the service is great and the wine selection continually expands. ⓐ Rr. Jul Varibova 6 ⓣ (04) 222 2632
⏱ 09.00–24.00 daily

Otium ££ ❿ A small but elegant upmarket restaurant on a small street in the Blloku, serving well-prepared international dishes at good prices. ⓐ Rr. Brigada VIII ⓣ (04) 222 3570
⏱ 11.30–23.30 daily

ABA Twentyfirst £££ ⓫ An elegant Italian restaurant at the top of the new ABA Business Centre skyscraper where the food, cooked by international chefs, is at least as good as the views.
ⓐ Rr. Papa Gjon Pali II ⓣ (04) 450 1717 ⏱ 08.00–24.00 daily

Era £££ ⓬ A favourite among foreigners, Era serves up a wide range of Albanian dishes, pizza and wines, allowing you to sample various regional specialities. Not cheap, but often very busy, so book ahead. ⓐ Rr. Ismail Qemali 33 ⓣ (04) 225 7805
⏱ 11.00–24.00 daily

CLUBS & BARS

Charl's Bistro Hailed as the best lounge bar and alternative music venue in Tirana. Live music happens all summer from Thursday to Saturday, while the lounge bar airs 1960s to 1980s music all week long. The outside garden is the best place to escape the smoky crowds. ⓐ Rr. Pjetër Bogdani ⓣ (069) 202 2901 ⓒ 24 hours daily

The Code This popular pub serves Irish and local beer, plays good pop and rock, and is consequently always crowded. ⓐ Rr. Abdyl Frashëri ⓣ (068) 203 7854 ⓒ 08.00–01.00 daily

Lollipop Hard to miss, and the booming sounds of house and dance make this Blloku's most visited dance club. It is cosy and cool with sofa seating and live DJs every weekend. ⓐ Rr. Pjetër Bogdani 36 ⓒ 12.00–05.00 Mon–Sat, closed Sun

Radio A stylish bar decorated with old radios and posters, where Tirana's party-minded youth head to talk and relax while listening to good music. ⓐ Rr. Ismail Qemali 29/1 ⓣ (069) 28 4424 ⓒ 09.00–01.00 daily

Steelwings Even if you're not a fan of motorbikes, this very welcoming Harley-Davidson-themed bar is worth visiting for its well-made drinks, as well as regular karaoke and concert nights. ⓐ Rr. Vaso Pasha ⓣ (069) 202 2331 ⓒ 08.00–02.00 daily

Tirana Rock A great venue for gigs. Every weekend has a live-music event with a friendly and relaxing atmosphere. The music choice tends to be soft rock, jazz and occasional pop. ⓐ Rr. Abdyl Frashëri ⓒ 09.00–03.00 Mon–Sat, 17.00–03.00 Sun

THE CITY

Green Tirana

Green Tirana represents a selection of the city's best areas for enjoying a bit of Mother Nature, treating yourself to a breath of fresh air in a capital city and supporting the many small enterprises that make their living from visitors. Fortunately, Tirana is surrounded on two sides by a mountain range, which of course provides an ideal environment in which to enjoy the views, have a walk, pose for that killer snapshot or indulge in a traditional meal.

SIGHTS & ATTRACTIONS

Ibë

Ibë village is 5 km (3 miles) southeast of Petrela Castle (see page 95), just off to the left of the road to Elbasan. The road to Kame (see below) is narrow but paved and easily visible from the main road once you've made the turn-off.

Up until a few years ago, Ibë was a relatively unknown village along the Erzeni River, tucked between the canyon and the foothills above Tirana. The rough terrain upstream forbids human settlement, making the river crystal clear as it flows through Ibë. The area is well worth visiting for the remarkable 360-m (1,181-ft)-deep **Pëllumbas cave** (w www.shpellaepellumbasit.com), which can easily and safely be explored. Park in Pëllumbas village, just beyond Ibë, and ask around for the local guide Behar Duqi (t (068) 360 7843) who, for a small donation, will walk you the two kilometres along a newly made path to the cave entrance, where you'll be

GREEN TIRANA

○ *Glide above the treetops in the Dajti Ekspres cable car*

THE CITY

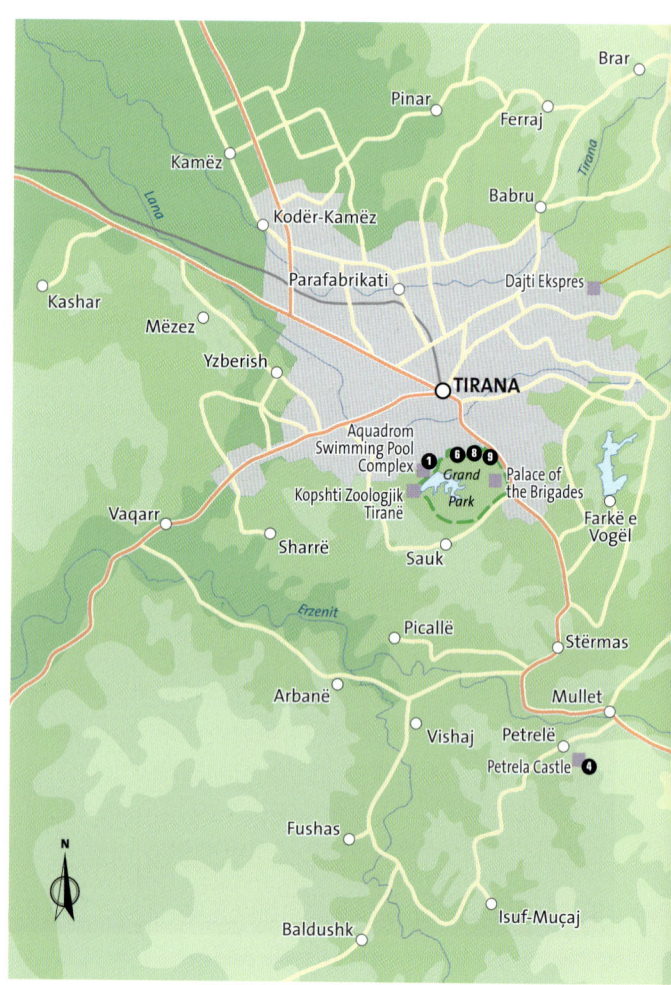

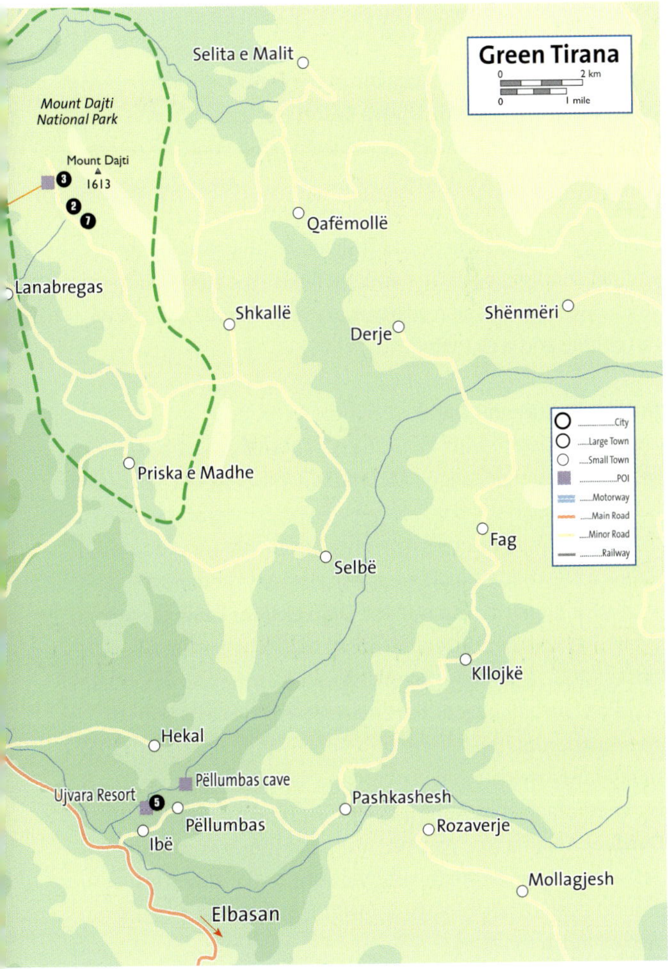
Green Tirana
0
2 km
0
1 mile
Selita e Malit
Mount Dajti National Park
Mount Dajti
1613
3
2
7
Qafëmollë
Lanabregas
Shkallë
Derje
Shënmëri
City
Large Town
Small Town
POI
Motorway
Main Road
Minor Road
Railway
Priska e Madhe
Fag
Selbë
Kllojkë
Hekal
Pëllumbas cave
Ujvara Resort
5
Pashkashesh
Pëllumbas
Rozaverje
Ibë
Mollagjesh
Elbasan

THE CITY

handed helmets. A torch is an essential item for viewing the wonderful stalactites.

Back in Ibë, you can take a dip in the cool Erzeni River or stop off at the lovely riverside **Ujvara Resort** (see page 98) where there's a restaurant, chalets and a swimming pool. The resort also incorporates the Teatër Park Kame, an open-air theatre founded by a Tirana University professor that is used for occasional plays and concerts. It's wonderfully relaxing to wander through Ibë village and the fields that surround it – you'll find that Albanian villagers are very friendly and always hospitable and welcoming.

Mali i Dajtit (Mount Dajti)

The entire eastern front of Tirana is flanked by the area's most beautiful mountain range – Mount Dajti. The peak, not particularly high by Albanian standards, towers 1,613 m (1 mile) above Tirana.

Apart from taxis or shuttle buses, there are two good ways to reach the mountain. The easiest, cheapest and most attractive prospect is to ride the **Dajti Ekspres cable car** (❶ (04) 237 9111 ❼ www.dajtiekspres.com ❸ 08.00–21.00 Tues–Sun, closed Mon). The main station is located at the end of Rr. Qemal Stafa on the outskirts of the city. A return trip costs 700 lek. The Austrian-built cable car is extremely safe and clean and the 15-minute ride, which culminates within the national park, is a memorable one. Alternatively if you'd like a guided tour, **Outdoor Albania** (see page 32) is a great group of young professionals who offer hiking, walking, and biking trips around Tirana. They provide transport, guides and a small packed lunch for a day trip.

GREEN TIRANA

Dajti, much of whose range is protected as a national park, is certainly the most popular and accessible wilderness area in the region. Paved roads offer pleasant walks across the length of the mountain, but the nicest trails are just behind the semi-derelict yellow building that you see as you exit the Dajti Express cable car station. Past it is a former military building which is fairly run down: just behind that is a trail head, which you follow to its first intersection. Here, you can proceed in either direction, but the trail to the left will take you into a beautiful, thick beech tree forest. From there you can hike to a nearby sub-peak with spectacular views in less than an hour.

For children, there are a handful of horses just outside the cable car station. These can be hired for a few hundred lek and taken for a trot around a field. At the cable car station there's the **Belvedere Dajti Tower** hotel (see page 37) with its revolving restaurant and the **Ballkoni Dajtit** restaurant (see page 97). Shuttle vans are ready to transport you (free of charge) to other eateries a few kilometres to the south. Walking is another option, and you can build up an appetite by following the paved road to the south. It's worth the trip as the views from these establishments can be quite remarkable, unless the city is veiled in smog.

Parku I Madh (Grand Park)

The Grand Park is the most convenient green area in Tirana and is accessible from both sides of **Mother Teresa Square** (see page 78). The easiest and most straightforward entrance is to the southwest: Dëshmorët e 4 Shkurtit eventually turns into Parku I Madh where they intersect at Rr. Adem Jashari.

THE CITY

◓ *Petrela Castle is Tirana's most well-preserved medieval settlement*

KALAJA E PETRELËS (PETRELA CASTLE)

In medieval times the flatlands of the Tirana valley were vulnerable to invaders, and consequently hilltop settlements were the main areas of habitation in Albania. Indeed, there are three strategic castles around Tirana, which were carefully positioned so as to be able to communicate with each other in times of warfare or trouble, principally by smoke signals. One of them, Petrela Castle, is one of Albania's best-preserved fortresses. Although there were castles of greater importance, such as those in Kruja, Berat and Shkodra, Petrela is no poor relation and was an important settlement as far back as AD 500.

The castle itself is perched on a hilltop on the southern foothills of the city near the Kërraba Pass, just off Rruga Elbasanit and only 15 km (9 miles) from Tirana's centre. The road to the castle is well paved and winds up through olive groves and well-kept village homes. Upon arrival in Petrela, there is a small town square with a few cafés, shops and vendors selling local handicrafts. At the far end of the square there is a stone path to the right that leads to the main (and only) entrance to the castle walls. The walk up is only a ten-minute trot on a well-maintained stone path. Strangely, the castle looks much larger from a distance. Once inside, the area is restricted to a small restaurant and café, with no more than a dozen tables on the castle terrace. There are, however, spectacular views in every direction. As with Mount Dajti, **Outdoor Albania** (see page 32) organises robust hikes along the Kërraba Pass.

THE CITY

This road leads directly to a **lake** (called both Tirana Lake and the Artificial Lake) and the park. There are well-maintained and clearly identifiable walking paths around the lake and across the dam that created it. The trails can be muddy after rain but are generally in good shape. The park attracts all kinds of visitors, though potential swimmers should note that they shouldn't use the lakes. If you do want to swim, use the **Aquadrom Swimming Pool** (see page 33), which, besides the pool, has a café and restaurant that overlooks the park.

At the far end of the dam is Tirana's zoo, the **Kopshti Zoologjik Tiranë**. Frankly, the standards of the zoo are offensive to most, and the animals' living conditions are mediocre at best. It is hard to judge whether the best course of action is to boycott the zoo entirely or to use the facilities in order to encourage local officials to raise their game. In terms of the wildlife on offer, besides the standard domestic farm animals, there is a wolf, an eagle and a few llamas.

On the eastern side of the park there are two **war memorials**. One is for British troops who died in World War II. This tiny well-kept cemetery is the scene of an annual ceremony held by the British Embassy for Remembrance Day in November.

The **Frashëri Brothers Memorial** is found just beyond the British graves. The Frashëri brothers (Abdyl, Sami and Naim) were nationalist leaders during the 19th-century Albanian awakening. From this location you can see a bland anti-fascist monument. Just visible on the far end of the park is the imposing **Palace of the Brigades**. Once the residence of King Zog, this is now a government residence and is closed to the public.

GREEN TIRANA

RETAIL THERAPY

If it's a retail fix you're after, you're most likely going to need to go back to Blloku for relief. The mountainous and green areas around Tirana have very little to offer in terms of shopping. What you may well find are roadside vendors selling homemade *raki*, olives and olive oil. In Petrela there are often villagers offering handicrafts for sale. Woollen socks and small carpets are a common offering in highland villages.

TAKING A BREAK

Aquadrom £ ❶ This café/snack bar overlooks the lake in Grand Park, just to the south of Tirana city centre. It's a good place for a coffee break or a light sandwich after a walk, or just a lazy day in the park. ⓐ Grand Park ⓑ 09.00–19.00 daily May–Oct, closed Nov–Apr

Panorama £ ❷ The perfect lunchtime restaurant on Mount Dajti, a comfortable 20-minute walk from the main cable station on a paved road. Panorama provides excellent Albanian and international cuisine at good-value prices, while the large terrace offers views almost to the Adriatic Coast. There is also a small playground for children. ⓐ Mount Dajti ⓑ (04) 236 3124

Ballkoni Dajtit ££ ❸ Perched on a cliff edge near the upper cable car station, Ballkoni Dajtit offers great views over Tirana along with well-prepared local and international food. ⓐ Mount Dajti ⓑ (067) 401 10 21 ⓒ 12.00–22.00 daily

THE CITY

Petrela Castle Restaurant ££ ❹ A restaurant that focuses mainly on traditional Albanian cuisine. The cheese and lamb dishes are fabulous. Make sure you ask the waiter, who'll be dressed in traditional attire, what the daily speciality is. The hilltop location also makes this an ideal place for a glass of wine at sunset.
ⓐ Petrela Castle ⓣ (069) 208 8138 ⓒ 11.00–23.00 daily

Ujvara Resort ££ ❺ Ibë village's only eatery, a restaurant serving delicious traditional meals, is found in a wonderful leafy resort that is home to chalets, a pool and a theatre. Perfect for lunch after visiting Pëllumbas cave. ⓐ Ibë ⓣ (069) 405 0200
ⓦ www.ujvararesort.al

AFTER DARK

RESTAURANTS
Dreri ££ ❻ Located just inside the entrance to Grand Park and serving both traditional and European cuisine, Dreri makes a nice break from the hubbub of Blloku. Service is good, the atmosphere is relaxed and the prices are reasonable. ⓐ Rr. Elbasanit, Grand Park ⓣ (04) 237 4745 ⓒ 12.00–24.00 daily

Gurra e Perrisë ££ ❼ Just a few minutes' walk beyond Panorama Hotel on Mount Dajti is by the far the best fine dining experience on the mountain. The ponds centred in the summer gardens serve as a trout farm, providing fresh fish for the kitchen, and the large beech trees shade you from the summer sun. Evening dining, inside or out, is first class and the wine list is impressive.
ⓐ Mount Dajti ⓣ (04) 236 3124

GREEN TIRANA

Juvenilja ££ ❸ Just past the Sheraton Hotel and skirted by a small pine tree forest, this castle-like structure has a large and very green garden. The food and service are top quality. For a real treat, ask for a terrace table facing the forest.
ⓐ Sheshi Italia, Grand Park ❶ (04) 226 6666 ⓑ 10.00–24.00 daily

⬤ *Teatër Park Kame in the small village of Ibë's Ujvara Resort*

THE CITY

🔺 Balcony on the Juvenilja restaurant

Sofra e Ariut ££ ❽ 'Bear's Lair' is sort of a Tirana landmark. Although the idea of attracting punters by using caged animals is not a generally accepted marketing technique with Westerners, the Albanians love it. The food is excellent, consisting mainly of traditional meat dishes. Definitely an experience worth having. ⓐ Rr. Elbasanit, Grand Park ⓣ (04) 237 2904 ⓦ www.sofraeariut.com ⓛ 07.00–24.00 daily

▶ The 14th-century Orthodox church in Berat's citadel

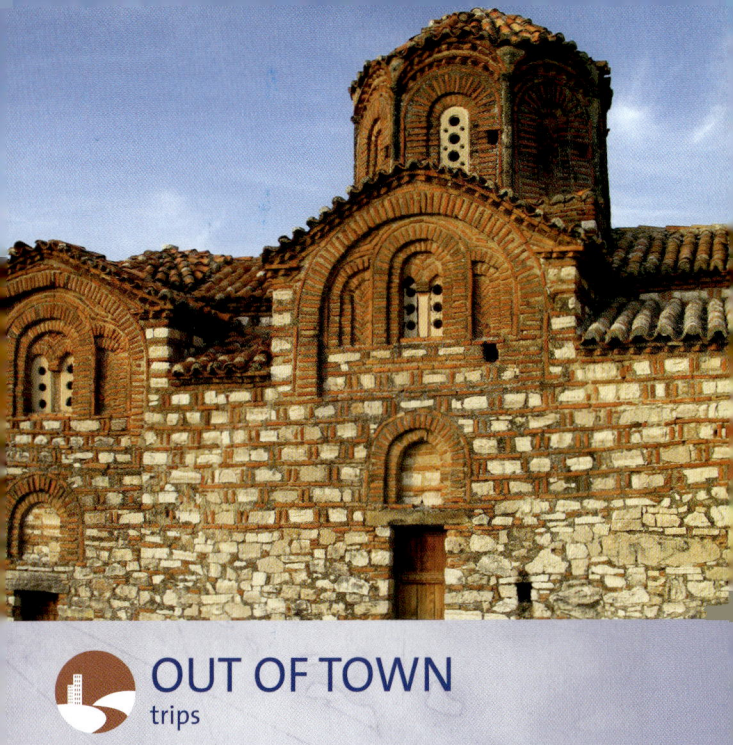

OUT OF TOWN
trips

OUT OF TOWN

Kruja

Kruja played a vital role in the shaping of Albania and was the state's first capital city in the 12th century. It is more famous, though, for having produced the most revered member of the Albanian family – Gjergj Kastrioti Skënderbeu, also known as Skanderbeg (see page 20).

KRUJA

Situated only 50 km (31 miles) from Tirana, Kruja is a perfect day-trip destination and is well known as a trading and craft hub of the region. An old **Turkish bazaar** (see page 107), a **fortified citadel** (see page 106) and two of Albania's most impressive museums can be found in this tiny hilltop settlement overlooking the vast Tirana valley. For those up for a steep walk, there is also

◎ *This ancient walled settlement was once the capital of Albania*

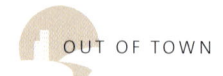

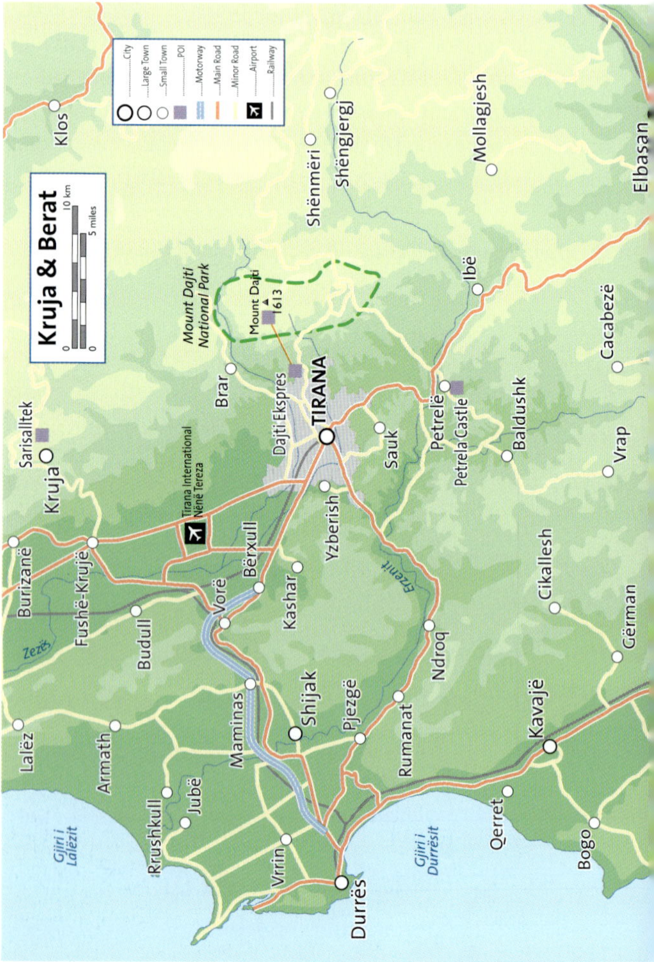
Kruja & Berat
0 10 km
0 5 miles
City
Large Town
Small Town
POI
Motorway
Main Road
Minor Road
Airport
Railway
Klos
Sarisalltek
Kruja
Burizanë
Fushë-Krujë
Lalëz
Armath
Budull
Zezës
Gjiri i Lalëzit
Rrushkull
Jubë
Vorë
Bërxull
Tirana International Nënë Tereza
Maminas
Shijak
Vrrin
Durrës
Kashar
Yzberish
Pjezgë
Rumanat
Ndroq
Erzenit
Gjiri i Durrësit
Qerret
Bogo
Kavajë
Gërman
Cikallesh
Vrap
Baldushk
Cacabezë
Petrelë
Petrela Castle
Sauk
TIRANA
Dajti Ekspres
Brar
Mount Dajti National Park
Mount Dajti
1613
Ibë
Shënmëri
Shëngjergj
Mollagjesh
Elbasan

KRUJA & BERAT

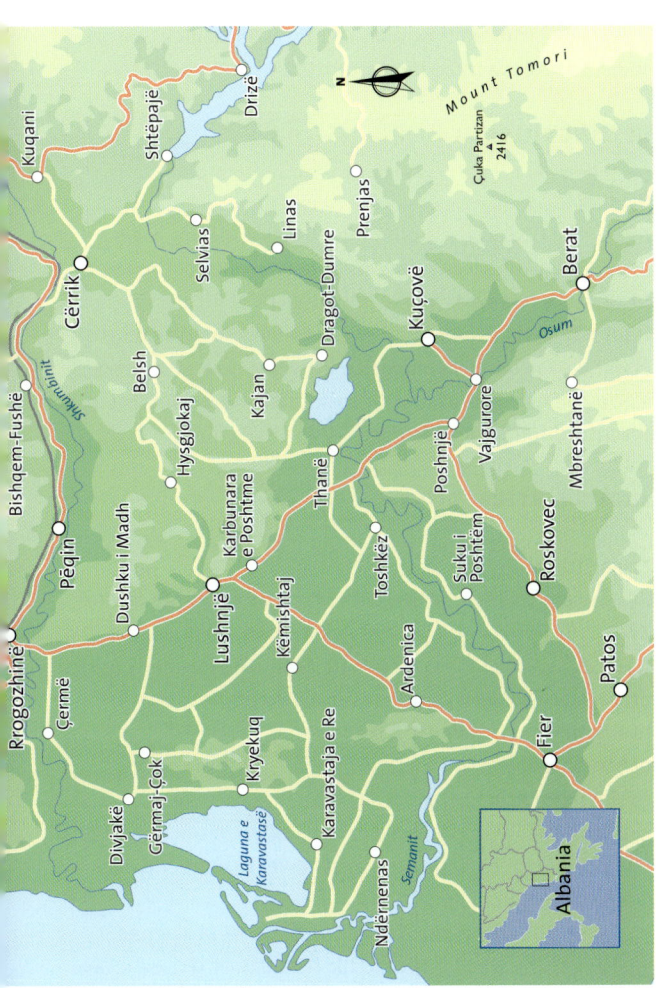

OUT OF TOWN

a Bektashi shrine on the mountain top at **Sarisalltek** (see page 108). The hike is a three-hour return journey on a good trail.

GETTING THERE

By road
Kruja is an hour's drive from Tirana. Buses and mini-buses depart regularly, several times per day, every day of the week. Most of these leave from the improvised station just behind the train station on the far north end of town. A single ticket costs about 150 lek, whereas a taxi ride will most likely cost between 3,000 and 5,000 lek each way. The local tour operators listed in Practical information (see page 135) run daily tours to Kruja.

SIGHTS & ATTRACTIONS

Kruja Citadel
Kruja was a strategic settlement as far back as the 9th century, and in 1190 it became the capital of Albania's first feudal state. Its citadel was built on a rocky outcrop and its elevated position offered long-range vision and even allowed smoke signal communications between the three main medieval fortresses of the Tirana area. This was the focal point of Skanderbeg's fight against the Ottomans. Ironically, after his death they drastically expanded the citadel and constructed many of the beautiful homes found there today. The clock tower is another typical Ottoman feature.

Although some parts of the citadel may be in ill repair, it's well worth the wander beyond the restaurants, museums and

DOLLMA TEKKE (BEKTASHI TEMPLE)

The Bektashi order is a 13th-century Sufi mystic dervish sect that originated in Persia. The similarity of the sect's belief system to folk and even pagan rites made it generally attractive throughout the rural Balkans. Thus, Bektashism spread in small waves through modest groups who were dedicated to a more liberal and mystical practice of Islam. In 1925, after the collapse of the Ottoman Empire, the sect was expelled from Turkey, and Albania became the world headquarters for this unique order.

Just down the stone steps and to the left as you exit the **National Ethnographic Museum** (see page 108) is a quaint little temple. The Dollma Tekke was built in 1789 and is one of the oldest such places of worship in the region. The temple resembles a mosque but its practices are drastically different. The job of caretaker, or *baba*, of the temple has been in the Dollma family for many centuries. The *baba* will gladly show you around the temple, and his wife often sells handicrafts on the steps at the entrance of the gardens.

the Dollma Tekke (see above) to see what 19th-century life here looked like. There are many tiny archways and side alleys that offer great views of the long valley leading to Tirana.

Old Bazaar

Whenever the Ottomans embarked on building or expanding one of their newly conquered territories, they focused very

OUT OF TOWN

much on trade and religion. Anywhere there's an ancient Turkish bazaar, there'll also be a mosque and, most likely, a water fountain close by. The Old Bazaar in Kruja is no exception. The remaining section of the 18th-century trading place was restored in the 1960s, and, although it only stretches 100 m (328 ft) or so, it is the only one of its kind in all of Albania. It's lined with souvenir, antiques and craft shops, plus stalls selling local arts and crafts. Do bargain with the vendors and ask for authentic, hand-made items so as to be sure you're not buying mass-produced factory substitutes.

Sarisalltek
There are many Bektashi temples and other religious sites scattered throughout Albania. Sarisalltek, on the mountaintop above Kruja, is one such site, possessing a shrine and a retreat house that is open to guests. You can drive the 7-km (4-mile) road to the top or opt to hike the well-maintained trail to the centre. The walk up takes about two hours; the canter down, half that.

CULTURE

Muzeu Kombëtar Etnografik (National Ethnographic Museum)
This rare example of a 19th-century wealthy Albanian estate gives an interesting peek into life during Ottoman times. Each part of the house is dedicated to a particular function. The relics, which include a lot of traditional attire, carpets and well-preserved wooden utensils, are in good condition and are intriguing. The ground floor segment is a perfectly preserved production line

○ *The National Ethnographic Museum in Kruja's old town*

for olive oil, flour and bread and all the other basic necessities for Ottoman nobility. ⓐ Kruja Citadel ⓣ (05) 112 225 ⓦ www.muzeu kombetarskenderbeukruje.com ⓛ 08.00–13.00, 16.00–19.00 Tues–Sun May–Sept, closed Mon; 09.00–13.00, 16.00–18.00 Tues–Fri Oct–Apr, closed Mon ⓘ Admission charge

Muzeu Kombëtar 'Gjergj Kastrioti Skënderbeu' (Skanderbeg Museum)

Constructed just inside the old citadel walls and opened in 1982, this is quite possibly Albania's best-staffed and most well-presented museum. Beyond the imposing larger-than-life statue of Skanderbeg at the entrance, the museum curators have done a convincing job in terms of presenting his importance in medieval European history. Documents, treaties and books all attest to the diplomatic and military genius of Skanderbeg, who is credited

OUT OF TOWN

with the unification of Albania's six main families via the 1444 League of Lezhë. It was from this point on that the Albanians presented a united front against the Ottoman army, and as a result defeated them countless times. The museum is a must

🔺 *Skanderbeg Museum*

KRUJA

while you're in Kruja. ⓐ Kruja Citadel ⓣ (05) 322 225 ⓦ www.muzeukombetarskenderbeukruje.com ⓛ 08.00–13.00, 16.00–19.00 Tues–Sun May–Sept, closed Mon; 09.00–13.00, 16.00–18.00 Tues–Fri Oct–Apr, closed Mon ⓘ Admission charge

RETAIL THERAPY

The **Old Bazaar**, which you'll see as you approach the citadel, is the retail centrepiece of Kruja for a large majority of visitors (see page 107). The Berhami father and son shop (ⓐ Pazari e Vjetër Derexhik ⓣ (05) 112 060) creates copper plates and coffee and tea sets, while the wool carpet boutique at the citadel end of the bazaar employs local women to hand-weave high-quality rugs. The Fazani shop sells classic souvenirs but also has the famous Skënderbeu *raki* and *konjak*.

TAKING A BREAK & AFTER DARK

Panorama Restaurant £ A large selection of good and inexpensive meals is on the menu. The interior of the restaurant is modern and tastefully decorated but the best seats in the house are on the terrace overlooking the citadel and bazaar. ⓐ Next to the Old Bazaar, on the opposite side to the citadel ⓣ (05) 113 092 ⓛ 08.00–23.00 daily

Restaurant Bardhi £ An eatery located inside the citadel walls beyond the Skanderbeg Museum. It serves good-quality international food at very reasonable prices compared to those in Tirana. ⓐ Kruja Citadel ⓣ (05) 112 772 ⓛ 09.00–22.00 daily

OUT OF TOWN

Taverni Veseli £ The Taverni is located on the right-hand side of the exterior of the main entrance to the citadel. It cooks up tasty Italian fare (especially pizzas), and the dining terrace has a perfect view of the Old Bazaar. ⓐ Kruja Citadel ⓣ (05) 114 416 ⓛ 08.00–22.00 daily

Grand Restaurant ££ It does not have the same views as the other restaurants in town but nonetheless serves some of its best food. The service is excellent and the outdoor terrace, a perfect place for an evening meal and a bottle of wine. ⓐ Kruja ⓣ (05) 114 557 ⓕ (05) 112 963 ⓛ 08.00–23.00 daily

Restaurant Alba ££ Praised by the locals as the best traditional Albanian restaurant in Kruja, this is located inside the citadel, just next to the Skanderbeg Museum. Lamb and veal dishes are the specialities here. ⓐ Kruja Citadel ⓣ (05) 114 390 ⓛ 09.00–22.00 daily

ACCOMMODATION

Grand Zeni Hotel £ A great-value, modern hotel with air-conditioning, TV and phones in all the (beautifully decorated) rooms. ⓐ Kruja ⓣ (05) 114 557 ⓕ (05) 112 963

Skanderbeg Hotel £ A Socialist-era hotel that has been modestly renovated since Enver Hoxha's days. It has 24 rooms, all with good views of the Kruja plains, and is less expensive than its competitors. There's a restaurant and bar, and rooms all have a TV and phone. ⓐ Kruja ⓣ (05) 112 329

△ *The Old Bazaar in Kruja is unique in all Albania*

OUT OF TOWN

Berat

Berat certainly ranks among Albania's most beautiful cities. It not only boasts some of its finest architecture, but is one of the most mixed communities in the whole country, being home to Orthodox Christian, Muslim and Vlach (a Romance-speaking people who live in this part of the world) communities. The city is allegedly one of the oldest in Albania, with a permanent settlement believed to have been established here in the 6th century BC by the Illyrian Dasaretes tribe.

Historically known as Antipatrea, it was captured by the Romans 400 years later. The town became part of the unstable frontier of the Byzantine Empire following the fall of the Roman Empire and, along with much of the rest of the Balkan Peninsula, suffered from repeated invasions by Slavs, Avars and other tribes. Berat thus has an incredibly rich historical heritage, much of which can still be seen and experienced. It's a fabulous place to explore for a day or two, absorbing its subtle beauty and fascinating charm.

Mount Tomori towers over the southeast horizon of Berat

OUT OF TOWN

On the main road into Berat you'll find the **Berat Information Centre**. It has maps and guidebooks and offers both guided and audio tours of the city. It also has a complete list of private accommodation available for traditional (and usually less expensive) home stays. ⓐ Mangalem ⓣ (03) 238 500 ⓔ beratinformation@yahoo.com

GETTING THERE

By road
Although Berat is only 122 km (76 miles) from Tirana, the journey usually takes a minimum of two and a half hours. For those interested in trying out public transport, buses leave regularly from 21 Dhjetori Square in Tirana, and tickets cost 400 lek one-way. Mini-buses, a more reliable form of transport, leave from the large bread factory on the ring road. One-way tickets are only 50 lek more than the bus.

SIGHTS & ATTRACTIONS

Berat Citadel
The citadel, tucked high on the hill above Mangalem, has been the centre of life in Berat since well before the 13th century. It is still inhabited and is, in every sense of the word, a living museum. There are a curious number of ancient temples, churches and mosques here. It seems that each occupying family had their own temple of worship, which gave rise to the impressive iconographic artwork on the walls and ceilings. The most beautiful and well-preserved icons within the

BERAT

castle complex are in the 13th- to 14th-century St Mary of Vllaherna Church.

Çobo Winery

Utilising both technology and traditions from Italy and their Albanian ancestors, the Çobo family has placed itself among the country's leading wine producers. The winery and cellar are open to visitors and it is possible to purchase gift packs of both Kashmer red and their superb whites. ⓐ Ura Vajgurore ⓣ (03) 612 088 ⓦ www.cobowinery.com

▲ Berat's old town is a UNESCO World Heritage Site

OUT OF TOWN

▲ *Osumi canyon rafting*

Lagija Gorica (Gorica District)

The Gorica district across the Osumi River has traditionally been a Christian Orthodox neighbourhood, and its architecture and spatial design has made it worthy of national protected status. The district is easily reached by crossing the Gorica Bridge by foot and is best explored by wandering around the medieval streets.

Lagija Mangalem (Mangalem District)

This was the Muslim district during the Ottoman era. The whitewashed walls, a typical feature of Ottoman architecture, seem to stagger up the hillside, one on top of the other. This adds to the beauty of what is already a very picturesque area, with dozens of tiny stone footpaths winding through the closely packed district.

Osumi Rafting

The Osumi River winds its way past Berat and Skrapar into the canyons of Mount Tomori. It offers visitors the chance of a 13-km (8-mile) rafting trip, which takes about four hours and is of a level that should be within the reach of supervised children.

CULTURE

Muzeu Kombëtar Etnografik Berat (Berat National Ethnographic Museum)

Created in the late 1970s, the Berat National Ethnographic Museum provides the region's best depiction of southern Albanian folk culture. The displays are well organised and offer an informative picture of what life was like during Ottoman rule. They also

OUT OF TOWN

> ### MUZEU KOMBËTAR ONUFRI (ONUFRI NATIONAL MUSEUM)
> Named after Albania's most talented painter, the Onufri Museum hosts an impressive ancient iconographic collection. The museum itself is housed in the Church of St Mary, which was constructed in 1797 within the castle walls. The nave and altar areas are stunning (the altar, hand carved from high-grade hard wood, is among the best preserved in Albania). Apart from the ecclesiastical area, the museum has three main halls that mainly exhibit icons from the 16th and 17th centuries. ⓐ Kala District ⓣ (03) 243 022 ⓛ 09.00–16.00 daily ⓘ Admission charge

give an idea of how the family unit functioned and how gender roles dominated Ottoman life. Separate sitting rooms for men and women as well as washing quarters show every little detail of social norms of the day. ⓐ 13 Shtatori District ⓣ (03) 232 224 ⓛ 09.00–13.00, 15.00–19.00 daily ⓘ Admission charge

RETAIL THERAPY

Although Berat ranks among Albania's most beautiful towns, it is rather small and still quite poor and there aren't the shopping opportunities that you'll find in Tirana and Kruja. In the old **Mangalem District** (see page 119) and on the road up to the castle there are small shops selling souvenirs, handicrafts and some locally produced foods.

The Onufri National Museum holds Albania's finest iconographic collection

OUT OF TOWN

During the tourist season there will be many vendors within the castle, mainly local residents selling souvenirs and handicrafts. Feel free to bargain. There is also a gift-shop at the **Onufri National Museum** (see page 120), with lovely Christian Orthodox icons, woodwork and photo books for sale.

TAKING A BREAK

Piccolo Grande Amore £ A restaurant, bar and café rolled into one that does good Italian food, especially pizza. ⓐ 10 Korriku district ⓣ (03) 234 770 ⓛ 11.00–22.00 daily

Restaurant Onufri £ Within the castle walls, not far from the main entrance. It's the best spot for a coffee break or a drink and they serve tasty home-made dishes that are Berat specialities. ⓐ Kalaja Berat ⓣ (03) 230 661 ⓛ 11.30–22.00 daily

▲ *The citadel is one of many inhabited medieval settlements in southeast Europe*

AFTER DARK

Ajke £ Located in the Gorica neighbourhood across the Osumi River, Ajke serves very tasty traditional meals at good-value prices. Try any of the lamb dishes. ⓐ Përballë, Gorica District ⓣ (03) 234 034 ⓛ 12.00–22.00 daily

Castle Park £ Off the beaten track and tucked behind the Gorica area in a nice pine-tree forest. The owner was a chef in Italy and the restaurant serves fresh and authentic Italian dishes on top of the items on the traditional menu. They cater to vegetarians as well – just ask. ⓐ Rr. Berat-Përmet (1.5 km/1 mile from Berat on the road to Përmet) ⓣ (03) 235 385 ⓦ www.castle-park.com ⓛ 11.00–22.00 daily

Mangalem Restaurant £ Serves Berat's best traditional dishes, and the terrace has a spectacular view of Mount Tomori. ⓐ Mangalem District ⓣ (03) 232 093 ⓛ 11.00–22.00 daily

Restaurant Palma ££ A slightly more expensive restaurant on the Osumi River, just across the street from the Mangalem District. The menu offers both international and local cuisine and has a decent wine selection. ⓐ Mangalem District ⓣ (03) 232 143 ⓛ 11.00–22.00 daily

ACCOMMODATION

All information regarding private home stays can be found at the **Berat Information Centre** (see page 116).

OUT OF TOWN

Castle Park Hotel £ A very reasonably priced hotel with several rooms and a handful of comfortable bungalows. Rooms have air-conditioning, TV and phone. The hotel restaurant (see page 123) is recommended. ⓐ Rr. Berat-Përmet (1.5 km/1 mile from Berat on the road to Përmet) ⓣ (03) 235 385 ⓦ www.castle-park.com

Hotel Nasho Vruho £ Family-owned and operated, this B&B is a unique experience in the heart of the old Ottoman neighbourhood. The host is a great cook as well. The décor is slightly heavy on the wood, but the place is immaculately clean and neat. ⓐ Shtëpi pritëse, Mangalem ⓣ (03) 232 355

Hotel Palma £ A small hotel with seven spacious rooms and a bar and restaurant on the premises. All rooms come with TV, air-conditioning, phone and en-suite bathrooms. ⓐ Mangalem District ⓣ (03) 232 143

Mangalemi Hotel £ The first post-Communist accommodation option in Berat. The hosts are friendly and helpful and the rooms are basic but clean and cosy. All have TV, air-conditioning and phone. ⓐ Mangalem District ⓣ (03) 232 093

Residence Desaret Hotel £ Berat's nicest hotel. The rooms are comfortable and clean, all with a terrace view of the city. It is ideal for families or solo travellers on longer stays. ⓐ 13 Shtatori District ⓣ (03) 237 593

▶ Tirana's new airport is well connected

PRACTICAL
information

PRACTICAL INFORMATION

Directory

GETTING THERE
By air
Tirana has a newly built airport (see page 48) that is well connected to Western Europe. Although it is still relatively expensive to fly into Albania's only airport, it is by far the most convenient means of getting to the city. British Airways flies directly five days per week from Gatwick. Travellers from North America, Australia and New Zealand should fly first to a major European hub, and from there to Tirana.

The following major carriers all fly to Tirana:

Albanian Airlines ⓦ www.albanianair.com
Alitalia ⓦ www.alitalia.co.uk
Austrian Airlines ⓦ www.austrian.com/uk
British Airways ⓦ www.britishairways.com
Lufthansa ⓦ www.lufthansa.com
Malev ⓦ www.malev.com
Turkish Airlines ⓦ www.turkishairlines.com

Many people are aware that air travel emits CO_2, which contributes to climate change. You may be interested in the possibility of lessening the environmental impact of your flight through **Climate Care**, which offsets your CO_2 by funding environmental projects around the world. Visit ⓦ www.jpmorganclimatecare.com

By rail
Albania is not currently connected to any international railway lines. However, train services do exist between several key cities

DIRECTORY

within Albania. If you're travelling from southern Macedonia via Lake Ohrid, there are daily train services to Tirana from Pogradec. Albania's northern border with Montenegro has a crossing at Shkodra. The train from Shkodra to Tirana is a scenic three-and-a-half-hour ride. There are six daily trains from Durrës to Tirana (see page 54).

By road
There is no doubt that Albania has made significant progress over the past few years. The road system, however, is still under development and stretches of road may be unfinished. If you choose to drive from the UK, there are several options. Car ferries from Italy (see page 128) run to Durrës, and the direct road from there to Tirana is in fairly good shape. You could also

🔺 *Trains from Tirana travel to other towns in Albania*

PRACTICAL INFORMATION

try driving via Montenegro and crossing the border over to Shkodra from Ulcinj on the Montenegrin coast. The border road is decent and there is a new road from Shkodra to Tirana that takes about two hours to traverse. The Podgorica–Hoti crossing along Lake Shkodra is another possibility but can be rather confusing and there are 30 km (18 miles) of fairly bumpy roads from the border to the Shkodra–Tirana motorway.

Reaching Albania by bus from Western Europe is still not a viable option. Services do run to the south and east, and there are regular buses to and from Greece, Turkey, Bulgaria, Macedonia and Kosovo. From the tourist towns of Dubrovnik in Croatia and Kotor in Montenegro there are more frequent day excursions on tour buses. These, of course, will be more costly than a regular bus but will get you to your destination nonetheless. Tour buses generally operate only as far as the border town of Shkodra, but trips further south to Tirana and Saranda are increasing in popularity as Albania's roads and infrastructure gradually improve.

By sea

The city of Durrës is only an hour from the capital. It is the country's main port and the best way to reach Albania from Italy and Western Europe without flying directly to Tirana. Most ferries sail overnight and arrive in Durrës in the early morning. Ferries from Trieste in northeast Italy depart four times a week, and from Ancona three times a week. There are also daily ferries from Bari and Brindisi. For ferry schedules and links to the various shipping companies see ⓦ www.cemar.it

DIRECTORY

ENTRY FORMALITIES

Holders of valid passports from the UK, Republic of Ireland, EU countries (except Greece), the United States, Canada, Australia and New Zealand do not require a visa for entry to Albania. Visitors are permitted to stay for up to 90 days. For those requiring visas, different rates apply to various countries. Visa applications can be processed in a few weeks and should be submitted to your Albanian embassy or consulate.

UK 🌐 33 St George's Drive, London SW1V 4DG ☎ (020) 7828 8897 🌐 www.albanianembassy.co.uk

USA 🌐 2100 S St. NW, Washington DC 20008 ☎ (202) 223 4942 ✉ embassy.washington@mfa.gov.al

Canada 🌐 130 Albert St Suite 302, Ottowa, Ontario K1P 5G4 ☎ 1 613 236 4114 ✉ embassy.ottawa@mfa.gov.al

Customs regulations generally follow those of the EU. For precise up-to-date information contact the Ministry of Foreign Affairs of Albania 🌐 Blvd. Gjergj Fishta 6, Tirana ☎ (04) 236 4090 ☎ (04) 236 2084/5 🌐 www.mfa.gov.al

MONEY

The Albanian currency is the lek, plural lekë. The international currency code is ALL. The government revalued the lek in 1965 so that one new lek equals ten old lekë. Some people still calculate in the old currency, but don't let this confuse you; most vendors will be honest about prices.

There are plenty of bureaux de change around Tirana and all banks have foreign exchange. Avoid exchanging money in the street. ATMs are found in most areas of Tirana and are all linked to the Visa, Mastercard and Cirrus networks.

PRACTICAL INFORMATION

Traveller's cheques are generally not accepted and many establishments, including some hotels, will not take credit cards, so it's best to ask before sitting down to eat or making a hotel reservation. Although the dollar and euro are well received in Albania (especially in hotels, whose prices are generally stated in euros), most places require payment in lek.

HEALTH, SAFETY & CRIME
It's always wise to have travel and medical insurance when travelling to Albania. Be sure to bring any necessary prescription drugs with you as some essential pharmaceuticals aren't always easily found. Up-to-date tetanus and Hepatitis B vaccinations are recommended.

Some claim that the water in Tirana is perfectly safe, while others insist on drinking only bottled water. Be extra careful with street food vendors, particularly in summertime, to avoid any spoiled meats or cheeses. Hygiene in most of Tirana's restaurants, cafés and bars is up to Western standards.

Expect Tirana to be a generally safe city. Albanians take great pride in their warm hospitality and give visitors exceptional treatment. Crime against tourists is quite rare, with the exceptions of pickpocketing and petty theft. Pay close attention if you're in crowded areas or using public transport. Around the main tourist areas there will be a police presence, although police officers can often seem disinterested.

OPENING HOURS
Banks, government offices and professional institutions tend to start their day at 08.00. Traditionally Albanians work until

15.00, though this is changing now and many struggle on until 18.00, with a break between 13.00 and 14.00. For private businesses and smaller shops, opening hours are between 09.00 and 15.00, when a Spanish-style siesta goes on until 18.00. Many shops will reopen for at least a few hours in the evening. Hotels, restaurants and other tourist service providers keep long working hours throughout most of the year.

TOILETS

Tirana's conveniences tend to be rather modern, although toilet paper, soap or paper towels for drying your hands are often missing. Most of the new establishments that cater for tourists are well up to par with Western standards. Public toilets are few and far between. It is entirely acceptable to walk into a café or restaurant of which you are not a patron and ask to use the facilities.

CHILDREN

There is an extremely high acceptance level of children in Albania, and they are most welcome in any daytime establishment. Cafés and restaurants will cater to even the most high-spirited child. However, apart from frolicking in parks, there isn't much for children to do in Tirana. The **Dajti Ekspres cable car** ride (see page 92) will most certainly be the highlight of any child's trip, and there's an opportunity to ride a horse once you've reached the top.

COMMUNICATIONS
Internet
Many hotels and B&Bs provide free Wi-Fi Internet access for their guests. There are a number of Internet cafés.

PRACTICAL INFORMATION

Global a Rr. Perlat Rexhepi 13 t (04) 225 6306 09.00–02.00 daily
Net 1 a Rr. Nikolla Tupe 1b 09.00–01.00 daily
Top Net a Rr. Vaso Pasha 08.30–04.00 daily

Phone
Telephone communications in Albania can still be inconsistent. It is very expensive to call outside the country from a hotel or payphone. Happily, local calls are inexpensive. Post offices have international call facilities where you must give the operator the number, and then he/she will dial it for you, direct you to a phone, and you will be duly charged for the amount of your call. Albtelecom, the country's monopoly-hugging provider, also has offices in Tirana from where you can place international calls. Roaming mobile phone service is mediocre at best. AMC, Eagle,

TELEPHONING ALBANIA
The dialling code for Albania is 355 and the code for Tirana is 04. If you wish to phone Tirana from abroad, dial the international code then 355 4 and the seven-digit number you require.

TELEPHONING ABROAD
To place a call to someone outside Albania, dial 00, then the country code, the local area code (usually dropping the first 'o') and the telephone number you require. Some of the more popular country codes are: US (1), UK (44), Canada (1) Ireland (353), Australia (61), New Zealand (64), South Africa (27).

DIRECTORY

Plus and Vodafone all sell Albanian SIM cards for about 600 lek (€4), if you think that you'll need regular phone contact with the rest of the world.

Post
Albania's postal service is not the fastest. For postcards or letters, feel free to send them via the local post. They may take a considerably longer time to reach their destination than in most European countries, but they will most likely eventually arrive. For important documents it is wiser to use FEDEX or DHL services. Sending postcards and letters costs between 20 and 60 lek.

Central Post Office a Rr. Çamëria t (04) 222 6282
w www.postashqiptare.al 08.00–20.00 daily

Plenty of public payphones

PRACTICAL INFORMATION

ELECTRICITY

Albania has 220V electricity with standard European round-pin sockets, but the country's poor grid means that the voltage can often be considerably lower. UK appliances will need an adaptor, available from airports, travel stores and electrical shops, and US appliances will also require a transformer. Be careful with laptops or other sensitive equipment and be prepared for occasional power cuts as well.

TRAVELLERS WITH DISABILITIES

Very slight improvements to access have been made in Tirana but, as is the case in most Balkan nations, travellers with severe disabilities may find it difficult to move freely and safely throughout the city. It is best to go with an organised group and to be clear about your needs when booking hotels and restaurants. For general advice on accessible travel contact:

RADAR The principal UK forum for people with disabilities.
⒜ 12 City Forum, 250 City Road, London EC1V 8AF ⒯ (020) 7250 3222
⒲ www.radar.org.uk

SATH (Society for Accessible Travel & Hospitality) advises US-based travellers with disabilities. ⒜ 347 Fifth Ave, Suite 605, New York, NY 10016 ⒯ (212) 447 7284 ⒲ www.sath.org

TOURIST INFORMATION

Tirana has two tourist information offices; one in the airport's arrival hall (⒜ immediately after customs ⒯ (04) 238 4980 ⒧ 09.00–19.00 daily) and one in the city centre. Both can provide general information and hand out brochures and good-quality local city guidebooks with maps.

Tourist Information Center Rr. Ded Gjo Luli (04) 222 3313 www.tirana.gov.al infotourism@tirana.gov.al 09.00–19.00 Mon–Fri Apr–Oct, 09.00–16.00 Sat & Sun Apr–Oct; 09.00–17.00 Mon–Fri Nov–Mar, 09.00–16.00 Sat & Sun Nov–Mar

Good quality service and information providers include:

Albania Experience For local tours, car rental, reservations and general information. www.albania-experience.al

Albania Holidays For incoming service, hotel reservations and general information. www.albania-holidays.com

ATHS For a full range of services, including hotel reservations, car rental and tours. www.plazh.com

Destination Albania For custom-made tours, a tour guide service and general information. www.destinationalbania.com

No Limits For local tours and general information. www.nolimits-al.com

InYourPocket Up-to-date listings of culture, restaurants and accommodation. www.inyourpocket.com

Outdoor Albania For nature-based activities, including hiking, biking and rafting. www.outdooralbania.com

BACKGROUND READING

Chronicle in Stone by Ismail Kadare. A stunning work of fiction about a primitive Albania merging with the modern world.

Broken April by Ismail Kadare. A rare insight into the blood-feud system of the northern Albanian clans.

Ancient Illyria, an Archaeological Exploration by Arthur Evans. Explores the fascinating links between the Albanians and the indigenous ancient Illyrian tribes that once inhabited most of the Balkan peninsula.

PRACTICAL INFORMATION

Emergencies

Most emergency phone lines do not have English-speaking operators. If possible, seek assistance when phoning in the event of emergencies.
Ambulance 127
Fire 128
Police 129

MEDICAL SERVICES
Clinic
First Aid Unit Rr. Gjin Bue Shpata (04) 222 2235

Hospitals
Hygeia Hospital Tirana-Durrës highway km1 (04) 239 00 00, emergencies (04) 232 30 00 www.hygeia.al

Dentists
Dental Clinic UFO Rr. Kavajës (04) 224 0028 08.00–20.00 Mon–Sat, closed Sun
Tirana Centre Rr. Myslym Shyri (04) 225 7446 08.00–19.00 Mon–Sat, closed Sun

Pharmacies
Farmacia Blvd. Zogu 1 (04) 222 2241 08.00–23.00 daily
Farmaci Regi dhe Bime Mjeksore Rr. Deshmoret e 4 Shkurtit (04) 222 6759 09.00–14.00, 17.00–20.00 daily
Night Drug Store Blvd. Zogu 1 (04) 222 2241 24 hrs

EMERGENCIES

> **EMERGENCY PHRASES**
>
> **My bag/money/passport has been stolen!**
> Më kanë vjedhur çantën/kuletën/pasaportën!
> *Meh can-eh vjay-dur chan-tun/coo-loo-tun/pass-a-port-un!*
>
> **Call a doctor!**
> Kam nevojë për një doktor!
> *Cahm neh-vo-yeh per njeh doctor!*
>
> **Call the police!**
> Thirr policinë!
> *Thi-er po-leets-ee-ne!*

POLICE

Dealing with police in Tirana is not an easy task. Very few speak any foreign languages and they can often seem dismissive of problems. Call 129 to reach the police emergency line but do not expect to find an English speaker on the other end. Ask passers-by for assistance if you are in trouble; Albanians are kind and helpful people.

Central Police Station Rr. Sami Frashëri (04) 222 8152

EMBASSIES & CONSULATES

British Embassy Rr. Skënderbeu 12 (04) 223 4973/4/5
(04) 224 7697 www.ukinalbania.fco.gov.uk
US Embassy Rr. e Elbasanit 103 (04) 224 7285 (04) 223 2222
http://tirana.usembassy.gov

INDEX

A
Academy of Arts 31
accommodation 34–9
  Berat 123–4
  Kruja 112
air travel 48, 126
Archaeological Museum (Muzeu Arkeologjik) 81–2
arts *see* culture

B
background reading 135
bars & clubs *see* nightlife
Bektashi Temple (Dollma Tekke) 107
Berat 114–24
Berat Citadel 116–17
Berat National Ethnographic Museum (Muzeu Kombëtar Etnografik Berat) 119–20
Blloku (the Block) 28, 74
bus travel 52, 55, 106, 116, 128

C
cafés
  Berat 122
  Green Tirana 97–8
  Kruja 111–12
  Northside 71
  Southside 83–4
car hire 56
caves 88, 92
Central Market (Pazari i Ri) 63–4
children 131
cinema 11, 12–13, 30
Clock Tower (Kulla e Sahatit) 62–3
Çobo Winery 117
consulates 137
crime 55, 130
culture 18–20
currency 129–30
customs & duty 129
cycling 32

D
Dajti 92–3
Dajti Express cable car 92–3
disabilities 134
Dollma Tekke (Bektashi Temple) 107
driving 52–4, 106, 116, 127–8
Durrës Port 54, 128

E
electricity 16, 134
embassies 129, 137
emergencies 136–7
entertainment 28–31
  see also nightlife
Enver Hoxha 'Pyramid' (International Cultural Centre) 79–81
Enver Hoxha's residence 74–5
Erzeni River 88–92
Et'hem Bey Mosque 58
events 10–13

F
ferry travel 54, 128
festivals 10–13
food & drink 24–7
football 32
Fortress of Justinian (Kalaja) 62

Frashëri Brothers Memorial 96

G
Galleria Kombëtare e Arteve (National Gallery of Arts) 66
Gorica District (Lagija Gorica) 119
Grand Park (Parku I Madh) 93–6
Green Tirana 88–100

H
handicrafts 23, 111
health 130, 136
hiking 32–3, 92–3, 96, 108
history 14–15
hotels *see* accommodation
Human Rights Film Festival 12–13

I
Ibë 88–92
Internet 131–2

K
Kamë 88, 92
Kalaja (Fortress of Justinian) 62
Kalaja e Petrelës (Petrela Castle) 95
Kopshti Zoologjik Tiranë (Tirana Zoo) 96
Kruja 102–13
Kruja Citadel 106–7
Kulla e Sahatit (Clock Tower) 62–3

INDEX

L
Lagija Gorica (Gorica District) 119
Lagija Mangalem (Mangalem District) 119
Lana River 44, 55, 66
language 23, 27, 53, 137
lifestyle 16–17

M
Mali i Dajtit (Mount Dajti) 92–3
Mangalem District (Lagija Mangalem) 119
markets 22–3, 44, 63–4, 107–8
Martyrs' Cemetery (Varreza e Dëshmorëve) 79
Marubi Film & Multimedia School 12–13, 30
money 44–5, 129–30
Mother Teresa Square (Sheshi Nënë Tereza) 78–9
Mount Dajti (Mali i Dajtit) 92–3
music 18, 28–31
Muzeu Arkeologjik (Archaeological Museum) 81–2
Muzeu Historik Kombëtar (National Museum of History) 67
Muzeu Kombëtar Etnografik (National Ethnographic Museum) 108–9
Muzeu Kombëtar Etnografik Berat (Berat National Ethnographic Museum) 119–20
Muzeu Kombëtar Onufri (Onufri National Museum) 120
Muzeu Kombëtar 'Gjergj Kastrioti Skënderbeu' (Skanderbeg Museum) 109–11

N
National Ethnographic Museum (Muzeu Kombëtar Etnografik) 108–9
National Gallery of Arts (Galleria Kombëtare e Arteve) 66
National Museum of History (Muzeu Historik Kombëtar) 67
National Theatre (Teatri Kombëtar) 30
nightlife 28–31
 Northside 73
 Southside 86–7
Northside area 58–73

O
Old Bazaar 107–8
Onufri National Museum (Muzeu Kombëtar Onufri) 120
opening hours 130–31
Osumi River 43, 119

P
Palace of the Brigades 96
Pallati i Kulturës (Palace of Culture) 67–8
Parku I Madh (Grand Park) 93–6
Parku Rinia (Youth Park) 63
Partizani i Panjohur (Unknown Partisan Monument) 63
passports & visas 129
Pazari i Ri (Central Market) 63–4
Petrela Castle (Kalaja e Petrelës) 95
phones 132–3
police 137
Port of Durrës 54
post 133
public holidays 11
public transport 48, 52, 54–5, 106
Pyramid 79–81

R
rail travel 48, 126–7
rafting 43, 119
restaurants 24–6
 Berat 123
 Green Tirana 98–100
 Kruja 111–12
 Northside 72–3
 Southside 84–6

S
safety 54–5, 130
Sali Shijaku Ethnological Museum 68
Sarisalltek 108
seasons 8–9
Sheshi Nënë Tereza (Mother Teresa Square) 78–9

INDEX & FEEDBACK

Sheshi Skënderbeu
  (Skanderbeg Square) 64
shopping 22–3
  Berat 120–22
  Green Tirana 97
  Kruja 111
  Northside 68–70
  Southside 82–3
Skanderbeg Museum
  (Muzeu Kombëtar
  'Gjergj Kastrioti
  Skënderbeu') 109–11
Skanderbeg Square
  (Sheshi Skënderbeu) 64
Sky Tower 84
smoking 29
Southside area 74–87
sport & relaxation 32–3

swimming 33
symbols & abbreviations 4

T
Tanners' Bridge
  (Ura e Tabakëve) 66
taxis 55–6
Teatër Park Kame 92
Teatri Kombëtar
  (National Theatre)
  30–31
theatre 30–31, 92
time difference 48
Tirana Lake 96
Tirana Zoo (Kopshti
  Zoologjik Tiranë) 96
toilets 131
tours 23, 32–3, 106, 134–5
tourist information 134–5

U
Ura e Tabakëve
  (Tanners' Bridge) 66
Unknown Partisan
  Monument (Partizani
  i Panjohur) 63

V
Varreza e Dëshmorëve
  (Martyrs' Cemetery) 79

W
walking 32–3, 44, 92–3,
  96, 108
weather 8–9, 46–7
wine 26, 117

Y
Youth Park
  (Parku Rinia) 63

NOTES

ACKNOWLEDGEMENTS

ACKNOWLEDGEMENTS

Thomas Cook Publishing wishes to thank TIM CLANCY, to whom the copyright belongs, for the photographs in this book, except for the following images:

Alamy page 80–81 (Per Karlsson/BKWine.com); Kaspar Bams page 127; Destination Albania page 31; Dreamstime.com pages 5 (Pavlos Rekas), 21 & 43 (Attila Jandi), 40–41 (Ralph Paprzycki) & 125 (Tupungato); Diego Gilli pages 7, 16 & 17; Grand Hotel Tirana page 35; KF Tirana page 33; Jeroen van Marle pages 20 & 78; Vlasis Vlasidis/123RF.com pages 28–9 & 59; Alberto Vaccaro page 133; Wikimedia Commons pages 89 (Albinfo), 9 (A. Dombrowski) & 57 (Dori); World Pictures/Photoshot page 47 (Armando Babani)

For CAMBRIDGE PUBLISHING MANAGEMENT LIMITED:
Project editor: Tom Lee
Layout: Paul Queripel
Proofreaders: Sarah Loker & Michele Greenbank

Send your thoughts to
books@thomascook.com

- Found a great bar, club, shop or must-see sight that we don't feature?
- Like to tip us off about any information that needs a little updating?
- Want to tell us what you love about this handy little guidebook and more importantly how we can make it even handier?

Then here's your chance to tell all! Send us ideas, discoveries and recommendations today and then look out for your valuable input in the next edition of this title.

Email the above address (stating the title) or write to:
pocket guides Series Editor, Thomas Cook Publishing, PO Box 227, Coningsby Road, Peterborough PE3 8SB, UK.

WHAT'S IN YOUR GUIDEBOOK?

Independent authors Impartial up-to-date information from our travel experts who meticulously source local knowledge.

Experience Thomas Cook's 165 years in the travel industry and guidebook publishing enriches every word with expertise you can trust.

Travel know-how Thomas Cook has thousands of staff working around the globe, all living and breathing travel.

Editors Travel-publishing professionals, pulling everything together to craft a perfect blend of words, pictures, maps and design.

You, the traveller We deliver a practical, no-nonsense approach to information, geared to how you really use it.

ABOUT THE AUTHOR

Tim Clancy first visited Tirana in 1999 as an aid worker during the Kosovo crisis, throughout which he lived and worked in Albania. Returning in 2007 he found a vibrant city finally in transition after the many years of stagnation and political quagmire. Tim is a travel writer, eco-tourism consultant and environmental activist, who enjoys shedding new light and offering a different perspective on the places and people of the Balkans.

Useful phrases

English	Albanian	Approx pronunciation
BASICS		
Yes	Po	*Po*
No	Jo	*Yo*
Please	Të lutem	*Tay loo-tem*
Thank you	Faleminderit	*Fa-lem-en-derit*
Hello	Përshëndetje	*Per-shen-da-teeyah*
Good-bye	Mirupafshim	*Meer-u-paf-shim*
Excuse me	Më fal	*Mah fahl*
Sorry	Më vjen keq	*Mah vien kesh*
That's OK	Në rregull	*Nuh ragul*
Do you speak English?	A flisni Anglisht?	*A flees-nee Anglisht?*
Good morning	Mirëmengjes	*Meer-men-jess*
Good afternoon	Mirëdita	*Meer-deet-ah*
Good evening	Mirëmbrëma	*Meer-brem-ah*
Good night	Natën e mire	*Nat-en eh meer*
My name is ...	Emri im është ...	*Emree eem oohsh-tuh*
NUMBERS		
One	Një	*Nn-yah*
Two	Dy	*Ddoo*
Three	Tre	*Tr-eh*
Four	Katër	*Cah-ter*
Five	Pesë	*Pes-eh*
Six	Gjashtë	*Jash-teh*
Seven	Shtatë	*Shtah-teh*
Eight	Tetë	*Tet-eh*
Nine	Nëntë	*Nun-teh*
Ten	Dhjetë	*Dee-yet-eh*
Twenty	Njëzet	*Nn-yuh-zet*
Fifty	Pesëdhjetë	*Pes-eh-dee-yet-eh*
One hundred	Njëqind	*Nn-yah-chind*
SIGNS & NOTICES		
Airport	Aeroport	*Arrow-port*
Railway station	Stacion treni	*Sta-chee-own tren-yie*
Smoking/	Pirje duhani/	*Peer-iyia doo-hawn-ie/*
No smoking	Ndalohet duhani	*Nndah-loh-et doo-hawn-ie*
Toilets	Tualet/Banjë	*Too-ah-let/Bah-nyie*
Ladies/Gentlemen	Gra/Burra	*Grah/Burr-ah*